STORIES FROM THE
SALES
FIELD

www.amplifypublishing.com

For more information, please contact:
Amplify Publishing, an imprint of Mascot Books
620 Herndon Parkway #320
Herndon, VA 20170
info@amplifypublishing.com

Library of Congress Control Number: 2020923515

CPSIA Code: PRV0221A
ISBN-13: 978-1-64543-799-4

Printed in United States

This book is dedicated to all the fabulous sales professionals who were gracious enough to share their stories, lessons, and sales tips with all of us. May they have continued success in the field.

Thank you to my niece, Marie, for finding all of the great quotes, which help to keep us all motivated.

STORIES FROM THE

SALES FIELD

Navigating a Sales Career in

a **Post-Pandemic World**

DENISE HORAN

CONTENTS

Introduction

YOUR UPBRINGING INFLUENCES YOUR FUTURE

I grew up in a family of salespeople and entrepreneurs. There was my dad, my uncle, my grandfather, my aunt, cousins, and more...

My father and my uncle, both successful salespeople working for corporations, decided to give it all up and buy some businesses in the Finger Lakes in Upstate New York. It started with a marina on a beautiful lake. Then they added a restaurant, ice cream shop, and gift shop. Between the two families, there were nine kids, and we were all expected to work beginning at an early age. Everyone was expected to "promote" the businesses. And that meant selling boats, gas, fishing supplies, ice cream, and—my favorite—desserts at the restaurant.

I guess I really didn't know that I was in sales back then. I must have liked it because I actually took a part-time job selling cable TV in the off-season while in high school. But, of course, this was all temporary. I had no intention of doing sales for a living.

I entered college as a premedical major at a big university. I loved it, but I found it to be a bit stressful. Working in the emergency room at the local hospital was not a "happy" experience. And when my rat colony in my research lab got loose, I said I thought I had had enough.

I was close to graduation and had not applied to medical school. What in the world was I going to do? My father had mentioned sales, so of course I was not going that way. Kids don't listen to their parents in their younger days. So I went on to graduate school for a master's degree in business administration, concentrating on marketing. I knew nothing about business or marketing. Or did I?

MY FIRST "REAL" SALES JOB WAS TEMPORARY

After five years of college and with another year or so to go, I realized I needed money and some work experience. I contacted an employment agency to explore positions. I told them I needed a flexible job because I wanted to finish school. They mentioned a position they really didn't think I would be interested in exploring. It was a straight commission sales position for a new company, and my boss would reside in New York City, while I was in Albany. It actually sounded like the perfect "flexible" position.

My boss got me a small studio with only a desk, chair, phone, and phone book where I could work. He told me to call everyone in the yellow pages and introduce myself, and if they had potential business, set up an appointment. I did what he asked. And I found myself on the top of the sales team within a short period of time.

I graduated with my MBA, and everyone asked what I would be doing in my new career. I really liked my job and my company and really didn't want a new job. So I asked my boss if I could manage other salespeople since I had that new degree. I went on to be a district sales manager, a regional sales manager, and then the VP of sales. It was a great job for twelve years. I just loved selling, coaching, managing, and motivating others to succeed.

MOVING OUT AND MOVING UP ON MY OWN

They say all good things come to an end, and this position did as well. I went out on the search for my next great position. I called everyone I knew to let them know I was in the market for a new "adventure." A few of my clients asked if I would be willing to do some temporary sales consulting and training while I was interviewing. I accepted a few of those positions and then a few more.

Pretty soon I was too busy to interview for other jobs. I needed some flexibility with a baby on the way, so I decided my own sales consulting and training organization was a good idea.

I was so fortunate to work with many people in many different industries. I structured and restructured sales teams, trained salespeople, and helped many entrepreneurs grow revenue. Maybe I did find my calling after all.

LET ME TELL YOU A STORY—WHY THIS BOOK?

Over the years, my clients would ask if I was planning to write a book someday. And the self-development experts recommended publishing a book in order to raise my consulting practice to the next level. I had read many great sales books over many years. And there were so many on the market. I knew I had to pick a format that made the book stand out in the crowd and at the same time address the personality of a sales professional. What I mean is that most salespeople have a limited attention span for reading. They are often "verbal, social" people. That is why I picked a storytelling format that is easy to read in small doses. This was my favorite type of training format as well. The retention rate seemed much higher. People enjoyed a good story, a lesson, and an action plan for improvement.

This book is full of interviews with people who are top in their fields from many different industries. They shared great experiences and sales tips that have been proven to lead to success. In addition, they offer an action plan for those who want to learn how to implement new practices.

I wrote this book so I could share the talents of true sales professionals. The best ones have so many experiences to share. Enjoy their perspectives.

AND THEN THE WORLD CHANGED

Suddenly, the business world crashed to a screeching halt from a worldwide virus. Nothing was certain or predictable. Employees were sent home. Not much work happened for a couple of weeks as people tried to figure out how to save their businesses and protect their employees from harm.

Salespeople who were used to being "out in the field" found themselves home. There were "no appointments allowed." Of course, the phone and email were the next best immediate options. But people needed to quickly get productive and change their habits. Videoconferencing became extremely popular within weeks. Virtual networking events, clubs, board meetings, and sales calls were held on videoconferencing. We are a resilient society that truly wants to succeed.

I have been studying the new trends, new options, and great stories of business survival. Remote selling is not temporary. Many will choose that option long into the future. We all need to keep our options open and keep selling. The best will continue to use their skills regardless of whether they are in person, on the phone, or on video.

Enjoy these great stories!

1

NETWORKING, PROSPECTING, AND LEAD GENERATION

If people like you, they'll listen to you, but if they trust you, they'll do business with you.
—Zig Ziglar

BLOOMING FIELDS

Since starting to build her coaching practice in 2015, networking, prospecting, and lead generation had been nearly half of Kim's work. When you are a coach, it is so important to market yourself. You are the hunter of your own clients. As you grow your business, the percentage of time spent actively hunting should go down a little because you receive repeat business and more referrals. "I am now in my fifth year, and I am seeing so many seeds I planted blooming. But I will tell you, I needed to be patient. In fact, I almost went out of business doing all this marketing work and not seeing enough of a return." But then an amazing thing happened for Kim. Someone replied to her newsletter; someone called and said that they had seen her give a speech three years ago—yes, she did want to say, "*Where have you been?* What took you so long?" Someone became a client after participating in a low-cost workshop, and then it blossomed into group coaching at their office, then to a coach-on-call contract serving their employees on a retainer paid by the company. "'I saw you...' and 'I've heard of you...' are now blooming for me."

But Kim said her question really should have been "*Why was I not better at follow-up?*" Why was she not creating more of a system to ensure that her information was kindly making it through the noise of the world? Sure, she attended events, collected cards, gave speeches, but she didn't follow up the way you need to cut through the clutter and stay top of mind. "In my defense, I did a lot of professional development, but—you see, I am just making excuses. I now know that I must stay the course, follow a process, and not just plant seeds but water them, tend the weeds, water again, then watch them grow, cultivate the lists, improve the contact, and make multiple connections."

Kim proceeded to talk about joining a leadership group with twenty women who could potentially be her target market. She said she needed to get to know everyone, be professional, and build some long-term relationships before she asked for business. Fortunately, Kim was able to be a guest speaker for one of the meetings. This was a great way for her to share her talents without "officially" selling. Two new clients surfaced.

Kim learned that visibility was the key to her success. And that visibility came in many forms—newsletters, mailings, phone calls, clubs, and her social media platforms. It was not just about going to events and showing her face. Kim said she really learned the value of marketing herself across many platforms when the pandemic forced her back inside. Social media and mailings became important. Phone calls and videoconferencing forced her to really engage with people in smaller groups.

In spite of a rough time for many, Kim's business has grown substantially. She continued planting the seeds and is getting much better at watering and nurturing them.

LESSON LEARNED: "I was haphazard! I need to be more disciplined."

SALES TIP: The seeds you plant in all your interactions matter. Being true to the process can see you through. Consistency and authenticity. Never desperate, never pushy, never phony—simply be as authentic as possible and stay the course.

ACTION PLAN: The process *and* follow-up—network, mail, email, phone, social networking, free webinars, newsletter, and so on.

FINDING A WAY TO MEET

Charles was an experienced banker and considered himself to be relatively good at connecting with prospects on the phone. He was fortunate to work for a large, well-known bank with a defined target market. He said it made prospecting easier. They were given business listings with good data to use for their target list.

But as you know, there is always that one prospect you think may be a potential client whom you just can't reach. This called for creativity. Charles called a few times at different times of the day, hoping to reach the CEO, but had no luck. And the prospect's gatekeeper was good.

In today's world there is a great deal of information readily available to those who search for it. It was time to do a people search on the CEO to see what he could learn about him that may help with a connection. Charles explained that many people go to LinkedIn and check people's profiles. That sure helps, but what happens if the profile is private, or there is no profile? It was time for a thorough internet search on Google and other platforms.

Charles explained that he is often surprised when he finds more than contact information and a couple of press releases. And this time he was very surprised. He wasn't sure why he was able to access so much information, but he managed to find the CEO's cell number, the boards and charities he was involved with, and even his name on a golf league list.

Charles found a common link in all this information: a local nonprofit with an upcoming event. Charles registered for the event with the sole purpose of making an introduction face-to-face.

Lucky for Charles, the CEO was standing near the registration table when he entered. Charles introduced himself and asked the CEO what had brought him there, as if the meeting were a coincidence. A conversation began. Charles said that although they would not be doing business together, the success was in the connection. It was one prospect he could take off the list. Charles said that it is important to have a solid target list that is well qualified so you don't waste your time. Taking names off the list was important. No one should spend time on an unqualified prospect or one you cannot help.

Charles said the key to a connection is to find something in common, show up in their network, or make a call outside of regular business hours.

LESSON LEARNED: Not everyone is a qualified prospect, but elimination is good too.

SALES TIP: Find the common link that makes for a connection or a rapport-building discussion.

ACTION PLAN: Review your list of "suspects." Make sure they are qualified prospects. Investigate.

TALK TO STRANGERS

Emily, a young salesperson with about ten years of experience in various industries, explained the value of being a "hunter." She said if you are not out there building your contact base, you will never be successful.

Emily recommended that all sales professionals have a prospecting plan. Emily focused on three things that proved to get her good contacts.

Cold calling was always a great skill. She explained that you can't fear rejection and you must be honest and to the point. "It's about people helping people." And she had a clear strategy that worked for her. First, use your cell phone so your company name does not show up on caller ID. When you reach someone, tell them they don't know you, get right to the point, state the reason for your call, and ask them if there is interest in meeting. If they are not interested in meeting, thank them, and ask if you can touch base again in three to six months. Hang up, move on, and send them a LinkedIn invitation. It is important to keep a database of your network.

Emily talked about LinkedIn being one of her best tools. She said when you use it properly, you realize it can be a small world where somebody knows the person you are seeking. Emily looked at her connections and their connections for possible leads. She sent messages to her contacts asking for introductions. These introductions become warm leads and often lead to a quick connection and an additional contact.

Emily's third prospecting strategy was networking in her community. Emily said, "I am a parent's worst nightmare. I love to talk with strangers." She looked for events where she may not know anyone or know very few people. She was seeking to get out of her comfort zone and talk to strangers. "You just don't know whom you will meet," she explained. You may want to assume that others at the event are in the same boat as you. Ask someone what brought them to the event and offer your help. In turn they will usually reciprocate.

Her strategies worked. Emily tells the story of wanting to meet a certain lawyer but having no luck on the phone. She found that one of her connections on LinkedIn knew that lawyer. She asked for an introduction. Her contact sent a joint email introducing them. Within a day, there was a conversation. Successful connection!

LESSON LEARNED: Know the worth of your time. It's OK to walk away and find a better prospect.

SALES TIP: Use your network and build on it consistently.

ACTION PLAN: Go to an event where you know no one. And talk to strangers.

GIVE-AND-TAKE FOR A WIN-WIN SITUATION

Ellie and her sister Kathy were so excited to start their own custom gift company. They were passionate about designing corporate gifts that people would actually want to receive. But Ellie told me it was not all about the creative side. Ellie and her sister could not afford to hire a salesperson early on in the business, so they set out to market their own business.

With little sales experience, they decided they would go out and tell their story. They would paint a picture of a fabulous gift being delivered to a client. And they realized they had to tell their story over and over to sell enough business to pay the staff.

Ellie said that they were fearless. They would talk to anyone. They would go to networking events and promote themselves. And what they learned was that they had to give a little to get something in return. "That was what networking was all about," said Ellie. People wanted them to be interested and helpful to their businesses in return. It was "give-and-take."

Ellie went on to explain their prospecting strategy. It consisted of networking at events, calling people they knew for help, and referrals and making the dreaded cold calls. She said they had to be fearless, face rejection, and not give up before they got a face-to-face appointment.

Ellie gave an example of a typical call. She would spend hours calling New York City financial institutions. She would hear, "We're all set now." Ellie said she would kick up the passion and reply, "Oh no, you just have to see what we do. I will bring samples." The key for her was just getting in the door. The beautiful gifts sold themselves.

Ellie went on to say that she received a referral to an owner of a printing plant that sent wine and liquor gifts for many years. Ellie remembered saying, "What is it going to take for you to invite me in? I have something you will love." Sometimes you just had to get to the point and be bold and blunt.

Ellie and her partner, Kathy, added prospecting and sales to their daily schedule. They knew it was all about the revenue. The company grew, and they were able to hire a salesperson, but they told me it really was all about the drive and passion for what they were selling that led to success.

LESSON LEARNED: Love what you do and share the passion.

SALES TIP: Always do the right thing. Deliver more than you promise, and make everything look good.

ACTION PLAN: Devise a networking and prospecting plan. Tell your story. Listen to others. Provide referrals, and watch the payback.

2

RELATIONSHIP BUILDING AND MAKING CONNECTIONS

*How you sell matters. What your process is matters. But
how your customers feel when they engage
with you matters more.*
—Tiffani Bova

MAKE THE BEST OF A SITUATION

Reflecting on her past, Cindy talked about how she always had a way of being able to connect with others. She says maybe it was natural or maybe she was just lucky...

Cindy was a young, successful salesperson in what she calls a hot industry at the time—cell phones. She had borrowed her boyfriend's new Mercedes, put on a beautiful suit, and set off to see a client. The meeting went very well, and she was running late for her next meeting. She knew she was driving too fast down a rural highway, but she did not realize she was going 105 miles per hour when the state police pulled her over.

"Ma'am, do you know how fast you were going?" asks the cop.

"No, but I bet you do," she replied with some reluctance. The police officer went on to say he was going to have to write her a ticket. Cindy politely picked up her brand-new, state-of-the-art cell phone and asked if the officer minded if she called her next client to let them know she was going to be late. The trooper looked at the phone and her jacket with the logo and asked if she worked for the cell phone company.

Cindy knew the conversation had suddenly switched, and she had an opportunity to either get out of her ticket or sell a new client. Cindy asked the police officer if he had a phone of his own. When he said no but that they were looking to get them out in the force, Cindy handed him the phone to check it out. They began bonding over the new technology and how it would make their jobs so much better.

The police officer went back to his car and returned with a slip of paper. It was not the ticket Cindy expected but the contact name for her to call at the New York State Police. She politely thanked him and asked for her ticket so she could get on her way. The policeman said there would be no ticket but that she better succeed in selling the contract so he could have a phone.

Cindy felt very fortunate and returned to her office. She closed the large contract with the whole police force and got a few more referrals after that. Cindy knew she was lucky but says that sometimes you just have to seize the moment and take all opportunities that come your way.

LESSON LEARNED: Connect with people. Find common ground. Make the best of a situation.

SALES TIP: Almost anyone can be your next client or referral source. Start a conversation.

ACTION PLAN: Drive safely. But remember that the people along the way are worth a conversation. Make a plan to meet more people, and build relationships that will help your career.

GET OUT OF YOUR COMFORT ZONE

Sabrina had been selling for Aflac for a few years when she decided she needed to expand her network. She was involved in leads clubs and chambers, so a charity seemed to be a good place for her to explore. She was the "newbie" of the group, so the leaders asked her to present a prominent businesswoman of a large private corporation with the woman of the year award. Sabrina had no real public speaking experience and had never met the award recipient. She was so nervous that she considered making up a story to get out of this award presentation. It was even more stressful when she was told she had to read a letter from the governor of New York State and that over two hundred people were expected to attend. Just when she planned to make up a story about an injured daughter, she realized that getting out of her comfort zone in front of all these people just might help her career. She also realized that the "prominent businesswoman" was the wife of the CEO of her largest prospect. She knew that opportunities like this were the reason for her involvement, and she decided the stress might be worth it.

At the event, a nervous Sabrina brought an Aflac duck to the podium with her. She explained to Jane, the award recipient, that she hoped the duck would provide some humor and calm her nerves. She did not realize that she had made an immediate friend in Jane, who empathized with Sabrina and loved the duck. And the duck was the connection she needed to remain memorable to her new prospect.

Sabrina gave the duck to the recipient, read the governor's letter, and presented the award. A successful event!

A few days later, Sabrina received a thank-you note from Jane, saying that she was more excited about the duck than anything else. Sabrina realized the door was open for a call to Jane. Bravely, she called her and asked if there was a chance they should be doing business together. An internal referral followed from Jane, Sabrina closed the business, and she remained friends with the "woman at the top" for a very long time. Sabrina offered to speak at other events with a little less stress than the first event.

> **LESSON LEARNED:** You just may be rewarded when you step out of your comfort zone.
>
> **SALES TIP:** You are not going to get new business if you don't ask for the appointment.
>
> **ACTION PLAN:** Review your "personal marketing and networking plan." Add a new group, and expand your circle of influence.

FOCUS ON WHAT YOU HAVE IN COMMON

Tim recalled when he was working for a heavy-duty truck manufacturer and was heading to Tennessee to meet with a dealer. The people in the South did not have the same style as those in the North. Tim had learned over the years that he had to recognize and adapt to cultural differences, pace, and style as he traveled through the United States. He was reminded that he was going to have to adjust his regular presentation into a more suitable "southern" presentation.

Tim's boss, having learned of the big appointment in Tennessee, decided to join him on this promising prospect call. Tim explained that his boss was originally from the Northeast and was currently residing in Chicago. Tim also mentioned that his boss was a fast-paced type with a heavy focus on numbers and quickly closing deals. Tim knew if he and his boss did not "adjust" their typical styles, the sale would be tough.

After many years on the road, Tim knew that the best way to build some rapport and a relationship was to take his cues from his surroundings and the prospect's body language. Tim and team entered the prospect's office, and Tim noticed a large gentleman sitting behind the desk with his arms crossed. Tim knew this was not the most welcoming posture. Quickly he noted his surroundings: He saw mounted deer heads and fish hanging in the office. Tim acknowledged that they both liked to fish, and Tim saw the prospect relax a bit. Since he had more relationship building to do, Tim said, "Don't you hate when you are headed out to go fishing and your wife asks when you will be home? Why do they want to put a parameter on your day? Don't you then just want to stay out longer?"

Immediately Tim saw the prospect's body language change. His arms were no longer crossed; he leaned in to bond and commiserate with Tim. Tim knew he had broken the ice and was beginning to build some rapport. Unfortunately, his impatient boss blurted out, "Enough small talk. Let's get to business." Tim noticed that the potential customer sat back in his chair, folded his arms, and listened to the presentation. The prospect remained cold and distant, and at the end of the presentation said he was happy with his current equipment. He then showed them to the door.

Tim was last to leave. The prospect asked him to come back for a minute. "Tim, I can see us doing business together in the near future, but don't ever bring those other guys back with you."

Tim returned weeks later and closed the deal. The relationship strengthened and yielded more business deals for Tim later.

LESSON LEARNED: We are more alike than different. Find common threads. Connect with people.

SALES TIP: Be aware of your surroundings. Notice others' body language.

ACTION PLAN: Go to a body language seminar or read about the topic. Add this fabulous skill to your sales visits. Make others feel like you are like them. Bond.

BUILDING LONG-LASTING TWO-WAY RELATIONSHIPS

A banker for over thirty years, Roberta has a clear philosophy and strategy when building and retaining relationships. Although some sales professionals believe in not getting too close to clients, Roberta thinks that relationships strengthen the closer she gets to clients. She enjoys learning about people and their families and believes in the benefits of socializing outside of work. This philosophy stemmed from the days she was involved in the wealth management division of her organization.

Roberta believed she could not properly service her clients and help with their financial well-being without understanding them and their personal situations. She respected her clients, felt thankful to know them, and focused on maintaining an honest and dedicated reputation in the marketplace.

Roberta also had a great referral network of businesswomen and professional services people. She has been rewarded with some great leads over the years. One of those leads turned into a great success story.

She was having lunch with an attorney who told her about an engineering firm looking to buy out the ownership. The attorney mentioned she could introduce Roberta to the firm but that it might be too late in the game. Roberta accepted the offer, and she got a meeting. The engineers were reserved and explained what they wanted.

After the meeting, Roberta knew she needed to "do something out of the box," something that would make her stand out. She strategized with her boss late on a Friday evening and decided to move quickly that night with a note. She outlined in a sincere personal letter what the engineers had asked for, not just what they needed, and painted a vision of what the deal would look like. She got the business and remained attentive throughout the execution to be sure everything went as planned. Although some disruptions occurred during the buyout process, Roberta helped wherever she could. Shortly after the deal, Roberta left her employer for another job, and the engineering firm client followed her. Roberta helped the client with a subsequent merger and another change after that. Roberta explained that loyalty comes from building strong, long-lasting relationships.

LESSON LEARNED: Research and prepare when meeting someone new. Take an interest in the person you are meeting.

SALES TIP: Be sensitive to personal information. Use discretion.

ACTION PLAN: Don't just call your clients annually. Stay involved. Share relevant information. Make your own call plan.

3

ENGAGING THE COMMUNITY

Alone we can do so little; together we can do so much.
—Helen Keller

ENGAGING A TARGET MARKET AS A PARTNER

Joan needed a career change. Her hobby was photography, and she had always wanted to make her hobby her career. She thought long and hard about how she was going to get new clients. Why would someone want to give her a chance? How would she be different than other photographers in this crowded field?

Joan's background was in fundraising. She had worked with over one hundred nonprofits in her community. Those were her connections. Joan contacted all of those nonprofits, each one with at least one major event for which they would use a photographer. She offered all of them a free trial at their next event in exchange for a contract commitment for future events. Joan knew that a trial would get her foot in the door. She also knew that many nonprofits struggled for funding, so she prepared a special nonprofit package that included a discounted rate and fast delivery of the photos. In turn, Joan asked for her logo to be placed on the nonprofit's marketing material as an event sponsor.

One nonprofit that accepted Joan's offer was the Women's Employment & Resource Center (WERC), which continues to use her today. Through her excellent photography, she bonded with the executive director and the staff. WERC offered Joan a contract to cover two events each year, provide great photos quickly, and, when the days of social media dawned, post them online for all attendees to view. WERC listed Joan as a media sponsor. Her visibility grew over time. She captured the views of all WERC sponsors, attendees, and local businesspeople who supported this nonprofit. She received additional visibility in the newspaper where the events were highlighted.

Joan's visibility in her community soared, new client's surfaced, multiyear contracts were signed, and partnerships were formed. She had secured her target market of nonprofits and the business community that supported these organizations.

LESSON LEARNED: Give a little in the beginning to secure a strong long-term relationship. Be a partner, not just a vendor.

BREAKING BARRIERS—UNITING INTERNAL AND EXTERNAL CUSTOMERS

The sales manager for a large asphalt and cement company, Sheila knew she had to find a way to engage her existing customers. She was sure she had the solution when she realized that her customers would enjoy seeing the large trucks and quarries where their materials were sourced. Sheila launched monthly open houses at the quarry. These customer appreciation events started small. The salespeople hosted the customers, and everyone received a lunch box and a short tour. The events were successful but somewhat of an inconvenience for the operations crew trying to work around the customers.

Something was missing. Why didn't the operations team understand the value of having the customers on-site? Why did they feel the salespeople and customers were in the way? That's when Sheila realized that the operations people should be running the customer appreciation events. The quarry was "their" place. Sheila expanded the customer appreciation events to every asphalt and cement plant and invited the operations crew to take charge. The events became so popular that the lunch boxes were upgraded to food trucks. All customers and operations crews ate together, mingled in conversation, and built the relationships that the company needed with its internal and external customers.

The sales team wanted to rejoin the customer appreciation events, but the team knew that the operations people needed to "own" the customers too. The remarkable results of these customer events were threefold: the customers loved the events, additional business resulted, and the operations crew's customer service shone.

As time went on, the events continued, and salespeople returned. The internal relationships strengthened. The internal barriers were broken, and the focus was on the customer.

Today these events still exist and have only increased in popularity. Everyone looks forward to lunch at the quarry.

LESSON LEARNED: Team building will secure the salesperson's relationship with their internal and external customers.

SALES TIP: Engage your internal customers (operations and service departments) so your external customers are serviced.

CUSTOMER APPRECIATION EVENTS

The owner and primary salesperson of her company, Kathleen has lived through good and bad economic times. When the economy tanked in 2009, she was forced to get creative. After many calls to prospects and existing clients, she continued to hear the same thing: no money for training.

"You just can't keep calling people over and over who cannot buy services," she said. She needed to find a better way to kindle relationships so that when the economy recovered, customers would come back. The creative side kicked in and "customer appreciation events" launched. The customers wanted training, and the employees wanted to train, so every month a free training session was held for anyone who wanted to attend. Although the topics varied, the format was the same, and the events became a monthly breakfast club. Old clients, new prospects, and existing customers all gathered in a big room to learn something new about technology. They also had some time for networking before and after the event. The attendees "sold" each other on the value of this training.

The outcome of these events was huge. The prospects learned what the training company did, its style, and expertise. The company had a list of potential clients for its mailing list. The relationships continued to strengthen. The network grew, and the community benefited at no cost. No employees needed to cold call or beg for business. As the value of these events increased, the money for training returned.

Ten years later, the customer appreciation events continue. The company has doubled in size, the mailing list has grown more than threefold, the community benefits, nonprofits are welcomed, and the competitors have fallen by the wayside.

LESSON LEARNED: Don't hide away during a bad economy; get creative and keep "selling."

SALES TIP: Your network, clients, and prospects are important even when they are not buying.

ACTION PLAN: How will you engage your community? Plan an event or educational material, or help solve a problem. Get visible.

AN APPETITE FOR COLLABORATION

The managing partner of a graphic design communications firm, Lauren knew she had to "hunt" business to keep her firm alive and well. She explained that she is not a "salesperson type," but she is creative!

The goal was to meet new prospects and allow them to see the beautiful branding work her firm was doing for other companies. Lauren decided a monthly lunch club might attract some new faces to her office. She also knew that she had to offer something to attract these people.

Lauren and her team did what they do best: they "branded" the lunch club to make it a special community event that everyone wanted to be invited to experience.

The invitation was a napkin. The lunch plates were bright orange with a company lunch logo. Guests were invited to take these beautiful plates home or to their offices as a great reminder of the communication firm's services. The conversation piece for the group was delivered as an icebreaker in an ice tray envelope. The menu card had a receipt to take home that had feedback questions to return. Everything was perfectly designed.

Guests arrived for the lunch club and were seated with eight-to-twelve new faces from the local community. Most were perfect prospects for the host—marketing people or business owners who had purchased design work or websites.

After introductions were made, Lauren used the icebreaker questions to stimulate conversation and make the group more comfortable at their tables. The conversations ranged from short answers to more elaborate discussions about design, marketing, and branding. The host never sold anything during lunch. The group "sold" themselves.

Within a month or so, a qualified prospect who had attended the lunch club inquired about services. New business was generated from the relationships built in this valuable community event.

> **LESSON LEARNED:** Don't prejudge. You never know when a room of new faces can find something in common and help each other.
>
> **SALES TIP:** Sometimes you do not need to sell. Just put supporters together, and let them sell each other.
>
> **ACTION PLAN:** Plan a group networking event. It's better when it is on your premises. It makes it more personal, like inviting people to your home. They will be grateful and often reciprocate with business or a lead.

"BRANDING YOURSELF" IN YOUR LOCAL COMMUNITY

Owner and lead salesperson of a computer networking company, Lauren decided he must gain visibility in a crowded field. "If people think they have heard of you when you call, they are more likely to engage in a conversation," Lauren explained. He knew he did not have the money for a full advertising campaign in his target market, but he knew he could find a way to be "visible" without additional funds. He had a small fleet of cars that his technicians drove to service calls. If he put his business name on these cars, the target community would see them on the road and feel like they "knew" the company.

Lauren put his logo on the cars, including his personal vehicle, to generate name recognition and top-of-mind awareness. Then he thought of an additional strategy.

Lauren knew that his target market—small-to-medium-sized businesses—had to see the cars. Like Lauren, those business owners were out in the community making a name for themselves and often attending networking and charity events. He spoke with his technicians, and all the drivers agreed to arrive early at events or when doing business and park the cars in the most visible spots they could find.

Soon Lauren's car became a conversation starter at every event he attended. People would meet him and say, "Oh, I saw your car outside" or "Great spot, Lauren." Lauren even put a logo on his wife's car.

In addition to gaining visibility, his team learned that their reputation was important: Each was not just another driver. Employees gained a sense of pride and importance and had a way to bond with others. The sales have grown, and Lauren has added more cars!

LESSON LEARNED: Get over worrying about being a salesperson. Create and provide solutions, and be proud to promote in your community. People want to help others succeed.

SALES TIP: Don't sell an appointment. You are calling to talk about coming over to help them or educate them.

ACTION PLAN: Build a brand in front of your target market. Plan your strategy to provide value, education, and solutions. Set your goal—be involved. Use social media content, logos, ads, or whatever you need to create "top-of-mind awareness" in the right places.

4

GETTING THE APPOINTMENT

I think the number one advice I can give is—you just have
to start it. Just get your feet in the water and do it.
I learned a lot from just trying it out.
—Yoshikazu Tanaka, GREE

KNOW YOUR COMPETITION

Donna just started her new sales career working for a regional delivery company. It was a new entrepreneurial company with great potential. It was unknown to most people. The brand had not been established, and the two big competitors were household names.

Donna knew she had a competitive advantage because the service the company offered was an earlier delivery option that others did not offer without a heavy surcharge. The sale was not easy. First you had to find the real decision-makers—the people who cared to get the information to the clients quickly and reliably. If only she had the decision-makers' information. She would save all the phone calls it took to search out the right people.

Donna was sent to Boston to train with another young person who was showing great success early in his career. Aaron told Donna to be ready to work from 4:00 p.m. to 9:00 p.m. and to wear casual clothes with no logoed attire. It sounded a little odd to Donna, but she was told they were going to learn about the competition.

Donna and Aaron started out on foot in downtown Boston. The courier services were out making their afternoon pickups. Aaron explained to Donna that it was important to know the competition and to use the information during the sales call.

The first lesson was to take some notes on where the competition was going to pick up their packages. They followed the trucks to the downtown buildings and fol-lowed the drivers to the offices where the packages were to be picked up. At that point, they could take notes on companies with potential business and their location. That did not necessarily give them the decision-makers' names. Aaron casually spoke to the delivery people when they were in the elevator. Sometimes a few simple ques-tions provided the information we needed—"Who's your biggest client in the building?" or "Can we help you carry the packages to the lobby?" or "Who's the nicest client you have here?" The research project was quite fun.

There was more. They could stop in at an office and ask the nice receptionists, ready to leave for the day, to give them some contact names. And they could leave their cards and establish some rapport for follow-up calls the next day. "Call list ready." Phone calls made with valuable and useful information in their notes. Decision-makers or users known. Questions ready. Trial offered. New clients. Success!

LESSON LEARNED: It is very important to know as much as possible about your competition to be able to sell your company's value. Know your similarities and differences.

SALES TIP: Think about what information is needed and how you can retrieve that information. It may be public information, or it may require a bit of creativity. Position your product and service to solve problems or provide value to your prospect.

ACTION PLAN: Create a plan to learn about your competition. Your plan should include market research and speaking directly to your target market. It is so important to asking the right questions and be able to present your value.

USE CREATIVITY TO GET AN APPOINTMENT

Ed started as a technician in the service area at AT&T. Years later he moved into sales.

Ed had a prospect list he used for his pipeline, calling each prospect to set up an appointment and hopefully close the business in his territory. It was not always easy, and he had to be creative and not give up when rejected.

Ed had a large retail store on his list. He called numerous times to schedule an appointment. Each time he was rejected with the usual "we are happy with our current service." Ed was a bit irritated, especially since his boss continuously asked about this opportunity.

One day Ed had had enough! He decided he had to do a little espionage. He dressed in his old service clothes, showed up at the location, and asked the receptionist who had called for a repair. Of course, they could not find anyone (there wasn't anyone!). Ed patiently waited at the front desk. Finally, the receptionist took him back to the equipment area and left him there for the repair.

Ed proceeded to review their old system and wrote down notes on the current carrier. He managed to get all the information he needed to write a strong proposal. He reflected on the fact that he should not have been spying, but he would have managed to get all that information if they had just invited him in.

Ed went back to the office and wrote up a compelling proposal outlining better service at a cost that would keep them secure for quite some time. Ed sent the proposal to the decision-maker and planned on telling the client that the repair technician had provided the accurate information on his competition.

The decision-maker read the proposal and saw the value. Sold! Relationship solidified.

LESSON LEARNED: Sometimes it takes some creativity to close a deal or just get that appointment.

SALES TIP: Think about what makes you better than your competition and how you will present your ideas.

ACTION PLAN: Prepare a strategy for the prospects who have been lingering on your list—get rid of them and move on, or get creative.

DISRUPT YOUR PROSPECT'S THOUGHT PROCESS (TO WHERE YOU WANT IT)

Brian told me that early in his sales career he was taught to call a prospect, briefly introduce himself and his product, and ask a few questions in hopes of uncovering a problem they were having. He called it "focused, methodical prospecting." He would uncover a few leads and put them on a call and email cycle, hoping someone would come through. Brian realized he had a big prospect file and many notes, but his close ratio was low.

One day it dawned on him that he had to do something different. He needed to "disrupt their current thought process." Brian explained that most people are happy with the decisions they made and their choices. They did not want to think they could have done better. And most of all they didn't want to be told there was a better option.

He called his "disruptive thought process" a "prescriptive thought process." The key to success was to paint a picture of their current path, throw in a big obstacle, and educate them on the alternatives. He stated a great example. "Did you know that eight out of ten lawyers use x service; why don't you?" He explained that this forces the prospect's thought pattern to change. And often they are open to being educated about what their competitors are doing and what else is available to them.

Brian said he no longer searches to find someone's pain or problem; he goes right to them with a "disruptive thought" and offers solutions or what he calls a "prescriptive solution," educating them along the way. Brian also stated that this process allows a salesperson to sell exactly what they want rather than try to mold a solution for each problem that we "think" they have.

Brian said that not only did he become a better salesperson but he also cut his prospecting time in half and doubled his close ratio. He added that you must throw out the "disruption" and move on if it doesn't click. Find the prospects that "fit" you. You can always revisit them at a later date, when the timing is better. "A positive, forward-thinking momentum while prospecting leads to success."

LESSON LEARNED: The "ripple effect" is real. You must plant many seeds that grow into real relationships later on. The relationships you build are more valuable as time goes on.

SALES TIP: Take a proactive approach. Bring the prospect a problem rather than asking questions to try to uncover an existing problem.

ACTION PLAN: Prepare your plan. Know what your product or service brings to the table and what problems it solves. Be methodical in your approach. Present a problem, ask questions, take notes, and be ready to educate them and continuously bring valuable information until they buy.

5

ASKING THE RIGHT QUESTIONS

*Asking the right questions takes as much skill as
giving the right answers.*
—Robert Half

A PROCESS-ORIENTED APPROACH

"In the early days, I was told, 'Make twenty-five calls
a week, and something will come through,'" explains
James. That did not always happen. "There had to be
something I could offer, something that would spark
the client's interest."

James said he learned two important lessons
after years of selling. The first was that he needed to
always have a reason for calling someone. This meant
he needed good questions, needed to stay educated on
industry trends, and needed to focus on his own self-

development to be known as a true resource to his clients.

The second lesson, more specifically, was that he needed to follow a clear process with great questions that would help hold the prospect or customer accountable along the way. "'Can I stop by in two weeks?' doesn't work," said James. "You need a good reason to come in. This is all part of the selling process. This is what keeps you in charge of the sales cycle." And he goes on to explain that the process only works when you have great questions such as "I need to know more about what you will purchase and when you will purchase." Good questions and clear steps to follow kept the door open to multiple calls and visits. Gathering information, providing information, and learning about the client's needs held both parties accountable in finding the right solutions. Jim said it was often difficult to remain patient when the cycle was slow, but it proved to be a better strategic selling process than rushing the sale. James mentioned an example of someone who was a new salesperson in his office who got "lucky" and closed a huge deal early in his tenure there. James said everyone thought this guy was great by looking at his results. Not everyone was aware that he did not have to "sell" or cultivate this prospect. There was an unusual need, so the deal was easy. Unfortunately, that deal was not there the following year, and the new person never put together a process that worked. He was always looking for a fast sale, only focusing on the close.

"If you want to be in sales for the long term and be

successful, you must ask great questions using a process that leads to success, repeat opportunities, and a strong relationship." James did just that and earned a promotion to manager. He was able to share his wisdom with others and make his region a success.

LESSON LEARNED: One needs goals and a plan to be successful. Results-oriented processes focus too much on the final outcome. It's better to change to a process-oriented focus in which every step matters. It makes the questions you ask very relevant for a long-lasting relationship.

SALES TIP: You must have a clear process to stay focused on closing a sale that solves a problem. Rushing to close the deal can backfire and kill the relationship forever.

ACTION PLAN: Know your goals. Design a step-by-step selling process that includes all the questions you will ask to arrive at the right solution. Success will follow.

YOU JUST CAN'T ASK ENOUGH QUESTIONS

After staying home for many years raising her children, Beth suddenly needed to return to the workplace. She had been a nurse before her years off but did not want to return to that profession. She got lucky and secured a position with a medical software company. She said that they must have liked her since she did not have any software experience or sales experience. The company was like a start-up—they were building new software and trying to beat the competitor and get it to market quickly. "There was a lot of energy in the early days. Everything was moving quickly. There was little support for training or assistance. Maybe that was good for me. The only way I was going to survive was to ask questions. I asked my employer, the support people, the developers, the prospects, the clients, and the users. I visited the facilities that were using the products. It was the only way I was going to be good at my job and be a resource to the clients," Beth explained.

She said maybe she has a somewhat inquisitive nature. All her life she has asked questions. She reflected on the beginning days at the medical software company and talked about her start in marketing. The company sent Beth to trade shows to generate leads. She didn't have one of those fancy card scanners to enter the contacts into a database. She knew these leads were valuable and called every one of them after the show to follow up by asking questions. The personal touch was far better than sending a mailing to a database of people.

Asking questions remained Beth's selling advantage as she moved into online demonstrations. "Software was hard enough to learn. It was even harder to teach." The only way to succeed was to continuously ask questions that allowed her to demo the relevant information. Beth could relate better with the clients by learning her product's features and the client's needs and putting it all together.

Beth went on to say that she also learned that no one is perfect, and the best way to get around a blunder is to find humor in it. She said she was embarrassed to share a story but thought it just may help someone who works too hard on perfection. Beth went on to tell a story about presenting to the Hospital Association to a table of executive men. She was nervous. Her product specialist had briefed her on what she had to cover. Her mind was full, and she was speaking quickly to get everything out in the allotted time frame. Someone asked about data collection. Beth quickly answered, "Don't worry—it's easy. You just have to load the data on a floppy dick [instead of disc]." Yikes! Now what? Instead of stopping there, she proceeded to continue the humor by saying, "Or if you are in Australia, you can load the data onto a 'stiffy.'" By then she had the room laughing. She poked fun at herself and continued. Beth said that you need to embrace humor when you know you can't take something back.

Beth continued to do well at her position. She ended by saying that she attributed her success to asking great questions and finding humor in her workday.

LESSON LEARNED: Embrace humor. Keep your cool and don't let them see you sweat. Nothing's perfect.

SALES TIP: Know your product inside and out so you are the resource the client needs. Provide valuable information by asking questions all the time—of the clients and of the product specialists.

WHAT NOT TO ASK

Michael and his wife started a business helping homeowners set up and repair heating, cooling, and technology —a multifaceted business. In other words, they would often get a job and see more opportunity for additional services in the same house. Asking questions seemed to be the best way to uncover any additional services they may need. "But sometimes too many questions is the wrong way to go..."

Michael said that they had been in business about four years or so. Things were going very well. He thought they really were good at what they did, and he was proud of the relationships he had built with his clients. He always asked more questions, searching for additional work. And then he stopped. He realized he really had to think about what he should ask clients.

Michael was hired by an architect overseeing new home construction for a prominent CEO in the area. The architect was the liaison between the homeowner and him, but one day Michael had the attention of the CEO. He boldly made a recommendation. "You know your garage is close to the master suite, so you may want to install a light switch close to your bed so you can flip the lights off from there instead of getting up and walking to another area."

Michael was proud of his "brilliant" idea until the homeowner said, "I have worked many years to be worth millions of dollars, and I think I will leave the lights on." Michael suddenly learned that what was important to him may not be important or good for the client.

Michael thought he had learned his lesson on how to deal with clients, but it seemed he needed more experience to realize that too many questions may not be the right strategy to follow. He was very excited to get a new client near a racetrack. The client was building a second home as his summer party house. Michael was told he wanted it to be high tech, with great audio-video capabilities. Michael was also told that he had been hired to investigate the wiring that had already been available during the building process. When he finished the job, he was asked to submit a proposal for the audio-video work. The owner said he already had someone in mind for that work. The owner pulled out a stack of cash to pay Michael to be finished with their engagement. But Michael thought he would try to build some rapport with him in hopes he would get additional business. Michael simply asked, "So, what do you do for a living?"

The customer, stone cold, said, "Never ask that question again."

Michael said he changed after that time. He no longer asked lifestyle questions, slowed down his rapport building, and waited for the client to speak first.

Michael's business flourished over the next twenty years, as he no longer asked too many personal questions.

> **LESSON LEARNED:** Don't assume that you always know what is best for the client.
>
> **SALES TIP:** You don't need to be "friends" with everyone.
>
> **ACTION PLAN:** Beware of questions you ask. Think first. Put yourself in the customer's shoes.

ARE YOU LEAVING MONEY ON THE TABLE?

Not-for-profit entities live and die by their sponsors and donations. Typically, the business development representative acts like the organization's salesperson. Sabrina, a seasoned salesperson, accepted a job as a theater's business development representative. She explained how important it is to use your sales skills even in the charity world.

Sabrina read that a bar and restaurant was opening a new location in the city that housed their theater. This would be their third location in the region. Of course, she knew that they would want some of the theater traffic.

As every good salesperson does, she called for an appointment. The owner agreed to see her. On her way to the appointment, she made a judgment call that a simple bar and restaurant probably doesn't have much money for sponsorships, so she decided to stretch a little and ask for $10,000. At least that would get their name on a plate in the theater.

The relationship and rapport building were going quite well. Sabrina learned that the owner's daughter was a "theater kid," and their family really enjoyed theater and entertainment. So Sabrina boldly asked if the restaurant *could* afford a small donation of $10,000. And then the surprise answer—the owner said, "What can I get for $25,000?"

Sabrina said, "I gladly closed the deal but left there very mad at myself. I did not research the company, the owners, and their past giving patterns. I did not ask what they *wanted* to give. I did not ask any questions." She proceeded to say that she learned a big lesson. She vowed to prepare and ask questions from then on.

Fortunately, the restaurant was a good sponsor and continued to sponsor the theater. Sabrina closed the business and learned a valuable lesson.

LESSON LEARNED: Do not assume anything. Inquire.

SALES TIP: Prepare for your calls—research the organization and prepare your questions. Asking is better than telling.

ACTION PLAN: Add questions throughout your sales process.

"TRADE ONLY" TRANSFORMS INTO "TOTAL TRUST"

Georgia, a financial advisor for a top financial institution, had a small client in her portfolio. She asked her partner if he thought there was any potential for more business from this gentleman. Her partner told her not to waste her time, because she wasn't going to get anywhere with him. He was only interested in making a few trades. She told her partner that she wanted to give the relationship a try and if nothing came of it, she would move on.

Georgia thought about the questions she would ask him and how she could develop the relationship to increase the business he gave her organization. Georgia knew she needed to ask the right questions and build some credibility and trust with this gentleman.

She built a good rapport with this client over the first few meetings. She asked a few questions to get her client thinking about the future. And when the timing was right, she asked the client what would happen when he passed on. Would his wife and children be taken care of? Did he know about how a trust worked?

The client called a week later to set up another meeting with Georgia. This time he had a list of questions. Georgia found out he wanted to set up a trust for the family. He also wanted to increase his life insurance.

Georgia was very excited when the gentleman planned for the entire family and made sure his wife was taken care of upon his departure. Georgia asked more questions to help complete the full strategy. "Who will control the distribution of money in the estate?" The magic question landed Georgia a full financial planning client with a personal trust, a distribution plan, and additional life insurance. Georgia and her client were able to plan the entire estate strategy before death. Her firm managed the entire estate, all the assets, tax issues, and the cash distributions to his wife.

Georgia knew the questions she asked along the way would be the key to their future relationship.

LESSON LEARNED: Your client must trust you and value your relationship. It is important to learn about their desires and needs. "It's about what is best for the client, not what is best for you personally."

SALES TIP: All salespeople need to focus on their revenue goals. That alone is not enough to be successful in the long term. The relationship, the trust you earn, and interest in the client's desires are crucial.

ACTION PLAN: Optimize and maximize all your calls and meetings. Have a good reason for the call. And keep asking good questions so the client is involved.

DIG DEEPER

Brian was a software sales representative for many years. He explained that many software salespeople sold by calling people on the phone and securing demos. He said that alone did not make one successful. There was more to it!

Brian went on to talk about his sales process and the keys to his success. First, he mentioned the sales team was fortunate to have a strong marketing department that was focused on bringing the salespeople the leads they desired. Once he received a lead, he made the phone call. For Brian, it was not just securing the demo; it was asking the right questions to qualify the prospect's intentions. He would ask many questions to learn about the prospect's business and how the software would benefit them. He would also ask about the management team and the users of the software. He went on to say that the buy-in was bigger than one decision-maker. Failure was often attributed to the lack of buy-in by others involved with the software. His goal was to have multiple people at the demo and to hear everyone's questions and concerns.

Brian added that he explained the buying and implementation process to the new prospects. He also asked many questions to address any objections or concerns they may have had going forward. His comprehensive process worked. In addition, one of the popular topics he discussed was the 30-60-90 day check-in. After a sale was made, Brian would put the new client on his call list to be sure there was a smooth implementation with no buyer's remorse. He would again focus on asking questions to determine the client's satisfaction. He would also explain to the new client that their company had a referral program in which they could earn gift cards, a free month of licensing fees, or credits toward upgrades. Brian's target market loved the referral program and would "sell" him to others while they were at conferences and trade shows.

Brian said his favorite calls were the calls to thank new clients for their referrals or the calls to new prospects who had been referred by a happy customer. Brian said he not only thrived in his position, but he also did not burn out as quickly as the basic inside salesperson. He said his success was all about learning more about the buyers and addressing their needs by asking the best questions. Job satisfaction, solving problems, and good relationships all contributed to Brian's employment longevity.

LESSON LEARNED: The questions you ask a prospect are the key to a successful sale, referrals, and retention.

SALES TIP: If you ask the right questions you will know when not to give up on a prospect. If they are qualified, persist. Look long-term. Investigate by inquiring.

ACTION PLAN: Ask great questions to the decision-maker *and* get their management team involved in the sales process. Do not rely on one person. Sell to the group.

"TO BE INTERESTING, YOU HAVE TO BE INTERESTED"

"I went to one of my first appointments alone as a rookie. And I literally threw up on the desk. I talked and talked. I was so excited to tell him everything we could do for him. He did not even get in a word. Well, the gentleman fell asleep. He didn't nod off. He started snoring. And I was upset. Upset enough to knock on the desk to startle him.

"This appointment taught me so much. It changed my sales career."

Ted said that looking back on his early days as a salesperson, he saw he had not realized how important it was to get to know someone, learn about their business, and most of all ask questions. "Asking questions forces the person to talk about themselves, and we all know that people do like when someone is interested in what they have to say." Ted went on to say that he learned the importance of relationships. "Good relationships were about solving problems and helping someone. They were about asking questions and listening."

Ted continued to talk about showing interest in someone to get them to trust you and confide in you. The relationships he developed got stronger. When Ted built questions into his meetings, his relationships were often like friendships, and he found his close rates going up. Ted no longer had to spend all his time "presenting" and talking. He knew that his questions would lead to trust and reward him with new clients.

Many years later, Ted shared that his preparation for

a new meeting included all the questions he planned to ask. A back-and-forth conversation on how each of them could help the other led to many successful deals. The trust was built early in the relationship and strengthened every time they spoke. "Show interest by asking questions."

LESSON LEARNED: Relationships matter. They need to be cultivated and cared for to be meaningful. Talk less and listen more.

SALES TIP: When you go into an appointment with a prospect, don't look for the dollar signs—look for a problem you can solve. Figure out how you will help them achieve a goal.

ACTION PLAN: With so much being done online with videoconferencing, email, and text, you must find a way to show your human side. Make your plans to do or say something special to show you genuinely care about the client.

6

CLOSING THE DEAL

You don't need a big close, as many sales reps believe. You risk losing your customer when you save all the good stuff for the end. Keep your customer actively involved through-out your presentation, and watch your results improve.
—Harvey McKay

NOT ALL CLOSES ARE "NICE"

Mike had been selling fleet trucks for many years. He knew not every prospect would be open to an appointment with him, but he wasn't going to give up on qualified leads. After many years of prospecting for the right clients and not giving up on an opportunity, he explained that one time he wished he had given up.

Mike went on to tell his story. He began by saying that his wife, a prominent human resources consultant, was totally appalled by his story and wondered if he should share it at all. Mike said he felt a need to tell the story so that new sales professionals could become aware that not all clients are good people.

Mike had a large list of national prospects. They had been qualified, so he knew that each of them could purchase trucks for their fleets. He said it was motivational to him to check off the prospect every time he secured an appointment. Of course, there was always that one prospect who wasn't interested in meeting. Mike did not give up, and after his persistence won out, the guy said to show up in his office around 5:15 p.m. Mike was not happy about the appointment time but was happy to finally get the appointment.

On the day of the appointment, Mike decide to show up a few minutes early to make sure they didn't close the office before his arrival. He stepped into the reception area and sat down and noted how quiet it was. It did not appear that anyone was there, although the door was unlocked and all of the lights were on. Within a few minutes, Mike heard some laughter coming from the other room. So many things went through his head. Could there be something nasty going on in the other room? Should I leave? Oh, no, this guy is more of an ass than I thought. Before Mike could make a move, an attractive woman stepped out of the office in the back and told him that the prospect would be with him shortly.

Mike noticed the woman was adjusting her shirt and smiling at him. He was disgusted. "How am I going to deal with this unprofessional man? Do I really want to be here?" Time was up, and the prospect walked out grinning and seemed to be so proud of himself. He said,

"You must be Mike, and you are early." Mike apologized and followed him into the office. Mike had decided to ignore what he had seen and heard and just get down to business, but the prospect insisted on adjusting his clothing, obviously showing off. Mike was wrestling with morality versus making a sale.

Mike just couldn't help himself. He said to the prospect, "Looks like you are feeling pretty good about yourself. Really, now? How good do you really feel? Good enough to buy three trucks from me right now so I can just get out of here?" Mike said in retrospect he could not believe what had come out of his mouth. He had always been the quiet, respectful salesman, not the bold, outspoken one.

The prospect said, "Yes, I feel good. And maybe it's a good idea for me to sign the letter of intent and get you out of here. We are both big guys, and you have the passion to close this deal, and I want you out."

Mike thought about this bully. The longer he stayed, the worse it was going to get. So he handed him the papers and left with the signed contract. The deal went through, and the new client suggested that business was to be done over the phone. Mike was thankful for that. This was not what he called a great client relationship. And it definitely was his worst sales call. Mike reflected on the whole situation with disgust. He said that sometimes the sale is not worth celebrating.

LESSON LEARNED: Sales calls are not always perfect. Not all prospects are good people. You just may have to sell it anyway.

MAKE ALL PARTIES WIN

Tracy, a successful longtime real estate broker, received a call from the CEO of a local nonprofit. The CEO explained that she really needed a good sum of money to help the nonprofit's financial picture and said she had some land she would like to sell. Tracy met with her new client and realized that only about ten of the fifty-seven acres were good enough to develop. The seller was looking for $250,000, which seemed a bit high since most of the land would not attract a developer.

As any great salesperson would do, Tracy set out to call some of her previous clients who may be interested in purchasing a small piece of land for development. She knew that explaining this listing may not be so appealing over a phone call. So Tracy called a developer and asked if he had some time to meet with a local nonprofit in need of cash for land. Since Tracy had a good relationship with him, and they had done a couple of deals in the past, the potential buyer agreed to meet the seller.

Tracy knew the seller and proud CEO would help

the potential sale. The three met, and they toured the nonprofit and the available land. The potential buyer explained he wanted to help the seller but really only needed eight acres of land and was considering making an offer on that.

Within a couple of days, before any official offer had come in, another potential buyer called to say he was interested in all fifty-seven acres of land. Tracy had to show him the land since there was no official contract. They toured the land, and when Tracy returned, she found an offer from the first developer for $150,000 for eight acres. Oh, no—now what?

Tracy, with many years of experience, knew that everything is negotiable, especially when there are good relationships. So she decided to bring the seller and the two potential buyers together with her to talk about a deal they may all be able to accept. The seller explained her need for $250,000, the first seller explained his need for eight acres, and the second buyer explained his wish for all fifty-seven acres.

The two potential buyers asked Tracy and the seller to leave the room for a few minutes. Tracy was so excited that her plan was working! They all returned, and the two potential buyers explained they had worked out a deal. They would submit an offer for all the land, and buyer one would take the eight acres needed, and buyer two would take the remainder, and the seller would be receiving an offer close to what she needed.

Tracy talked about the win for all parties. This would never have happened if they had not all gotten in a room together without any attorneys present. Relationships matter.

Tracy has made "relationship selling" part of her strategy for many years. She is the owner of a successful women–owned commercial real estate business. And she has sold additional land to those developers, who appreciated her style.

LESSON LEARNED: Seize an opportunity. Look at its potential from all angles. Think of what everyone wants and have a vision for the ending.

SALES TIP: Make the deal a win-win for all parties.

ACTION PLAN: Continue to build strong relationships. Touch base with old and new contacts at least twice a year. Cultivate relationships that will bring repeat business. Add face-to-face meetings to your personal selling process.

THOUGHTS FROM A ROOKIE

Kate had returned from college early, in the midst of turmoil. No one knew how long this quarantine was going to last. She heard that her friends were losing their summer jobs, internships, and the job offers they had secured. She felt nervous that she would not be able to work and save money for the following year. A friend mentioned she should consider selling Cutco since it was a flexible job she could do at home. Kate had never sold anything before. She thought about the benefit of having some sales skills on her resume. Kate also thought about her generation's reputation for poor verbal communication skills. Maybe this position would help her verbal skills as well. With no job and a pandemic wrecking the economy, what did she have to lose?

Kate's first impression was that the training lacked engagement. They spent too much time talking about goals instead of educating the rookies on selling skills and product skills. Kate said, "I know goals are important, but I prefer to look at my long-term goals and add some short-term checkpoints to stay on track."

Although Kate was uneasy with all of this, she proceeded ahead and did her first demo as they had taught her. It was "cookie cutter, rough, not for me." She felt constrained. "When I started engaging with my potential clients, things changed. I started asking questions and learning about people's interests. I got rid of the script. I started closing sales and was a top seller my first week." She expected a little praise from the boss, but he seemed more concerned that she wasn't following the rules.

"I learned what kind of manager I didn't want. A manager can motivate you to succeed, and so can the customer. I learned the importance of asking about the customer's needs and wants. I also learned I had to earn a referral, and it was OK to ask for that later in the cycle."

Although she learned that this job was not for her and easy money doesn't exist, she got a new perspective on her focus and commitment to her career, not just a job. She made some money selling and got lucky and landed a paid internship shortly afterward.

> **LESSON LEARNED:** "I knew I had to develop my own strategy and style to feel comfortable. I also learned that asking questions was the most important part of the call. It's OK to do your own thing if you get the right results."
>
> **SALES TIP:** Think about your audience. Ask about their interests and match them up with what you have to offer.
>
> **ACTION PLAN:** Educate yourself on your products and services so you can provide value. And know your audience. Ask questions and prepare.

SOMETIMES YOU GET THE UNEXPECTED

Patty sold furniture for many years. She explained that the industry was very competitive. She knew early on in her career that she needed to network in the right places, build relationships with referral sources and purchasing managers, and negotiate by showing value, not just price.

Patty was proud to share the story of her networking skills. She said it was important for her to speak with economic developers, commercial real estate agents, and local builders. Her relationship-building skills were so important to receiving information early. Patty wanted to know when businesses were thinking of moving into the area, moving their businesses, or starting a new company. The furniture discussion often came before the official announcement was made to the public.

One of Patty's best networking, relationship-building experiences was when her commercial real estate agent contact asked if she was willing to help him confidentially install furniture into a temporary office and hold the secret for many years while a large company planned its move to the area. Patty's integrity earned her a great relationship with her referral source, a brand-new relationship with a new business coming into the area, and a very large client once the move was complete. This very large opportunity turned out to be a big, long-lasting client with years of growth and expansion.

Patty went on to remind us that her job was not only about relationships. In order to close deals, she needed integrity, honesty, and great negotiation skills—the skills that sold not only price but also value. It was a competitive market with slim margins.

She said she had one funnier story to share. She really wanted to work with a local hospital. She spent time building strong relationships with the purchasing people and earned her good reputation in the marketplace. As always, it still came down to the negotiations. She understood that good purchasing managers had to negotiate. The secret was negotiating by showing value. The profits were always being challenged. Patty listened carefully to what the client was asking for and explained she would be back shortly since she was going to give birth soon and was hoping to close the deal prior to maternity leave. Patty did not want to "give away the store" just to rush the job. She studied the client's issues, made some adjustments, and held tight on a few issues that were important to her boss.

Patty returned with a contract and sat with the buyer. He was pleased with most of the contract but asked about a couple of small parts that were not going his way. Patty said her strong relationship with him allowed for a discussion and some jokes. Patty told the buyer, "If you don't hurry and sign, I may give birth in your office." The gentleman laughed. Patty let a moment of silence go by, and then, perfect timing—the baby gave a big kick that was totally noticeable under her dress. The buyer stood up, shocked, and said, "OK, I will sign if you hurry up and get out of here before you have this baby in my office." Patty said this successful deal only happened because of the strong relationship they had built, one with mutual respect for each other's positions.

Patty happily took the signed contract back to her office, went on maternity leave, and returned to a happy client and a great story. Sometimes you get lucky and the unexpected happens!

LESSON LEARNED: Never give up, even on your worst day. You should celebrate or commiserate only for twenty-four hours and then move on.

SALES TIP: Know whom you are speaking with. Talk to everyone like they are a prospect or a referral source. People know people. Don't discount anyone. Be kind, helpful, and grateful.

ACTION PLAN: Follow up on all leads in a timely fashion. If you need more leads, meet more people, and find yourself a great mentor.

7

MANAGING
THE AFTER-SALE

*If you are not taking care of your customer,
your competitor will.*
—Bob Hooey

TOUGH CLIENTS MAKE YOU A BETTER SALESPERSON

Dan was a rookie salesperson for a delivery service. He worked hard to turn a new prospect into a regular client. He educated the client on the service value, the competitive pricing, and the personalized service he would provide. The client agreed to give him a ninety-day trial. "If all goes well, we can build a relationship," the customer told him.

Dan was taught that building the relationship with the prospect was important to maintaining the business.

But this guy was tough and didn't have time to build a relationship. So the trial began anyway. All went well at first, and then a delivery was late. Of course, the most important delivery is late.

A phone call with an apology was not going to be enough. Dan drove to the client site for a personal apology and explained how this would be addressed to ensure it wouldn't happen again. And when Dan got back to the office, he pondered how he was going to continue to sell value, even to existing customers. He realized "the sale" is never really over. He needed an after-sale plan to retain his good clients.

In the delivery business, there was a lot of room for error—an accident or a weather delay was common, especially in the big cities. The competitors were more easily forgiven with their big brands, great commercials, and on-time delivery records. So Dan decided his "after-sale plan" would include personalization (he was the brand), an on-time delivery report for review monthly with the client, and a regular visit to the location to help out on a busy day or to meet others who were involved in the service business. Dan explained that he realized that the tough clients actually made him a better salesperson. He learned about client retention, after-sale practices, and strengthening relationships.

As time went on, the relationship improved, and when the second delivery was late and the business was threatened, Dan had built a stronger relationship that helped to deal with the client. In fact, Dan and his client became friends, so it was OK that Dan tested his humor by sending over the video *Groundhog Day*.

The client laughed. Dan worked harder and smarter to preserve the relationship. The after-sale plan became as important as the sale. The relationship went on for years, and both parties benefited.

LESSON LEARNED: Never give up. It's worth strengthening the relationship. Sometimes a little creativity or humor helps.

SALES TIP: Always sell value and service. You are just as much of a "brand" as your product or service.

ACTION PLAN: Know how you will "secure" your client, even when things go wrong. Have an "after-sale" retention strategy.

THE MOST IMPORTANT PART OF OUR PROCESS

Miriam has been a recruiter for many years. Now in her own firm, she told me the most important part of her position was the "after-sale." So much happened within ninety days of the candidate accepting a position.

Recruiters have two clients: the employer and the candidate. The employer is the paying customer, and the candidate does not pay but must not only accept the position but also commit to that position and settle in. When the candidate accepts a position, Miriam's job kicks into high gear. The relationship she has built becomes extremely important. She has coached many candidates through the process of leaving their current job and transitioning into the next job. She has discussed how to give notice to the current employer and what may happen when the prior employer offers the candidate a counteroffer. And she must motivate the employee to focus on the new position.

Once the candidate begins the new position, the subsequent ninety days are critical. Most recruiters are not fully paid until this ninety-day period is over. It is Miriam's job to talk with the employer about a good onboarding experience for the candidate. She has discussed the training and welcoming that will be given in the early days. She has also discussed the candidate's expectations. It is important that the relationship begins the right way. Miriam calls her clients weekly to make sure the onboarding is working out well for both sides.

After ninety days, the relationship continues to strengthen. Miriam has called every employer that has given her business. She would start her calls with a thank-you. Soon after, she would call again to ask for additional positions and referrals. The next call would be an invitation to join and interact on social media. "Social media plays a big role now. It is a great place to post positions and engage with the community," she explained.

Miriam went on to add that she participated annually in a national *Forbes* survey that gauges "how we are doing" and rates the recruiters. She also sends quarterly survey of her own. Service, communication, and a strong relationship are the keys to success in that industry.

Proudly, Miriam touted her strong ratings by *Forbes* magazine and explained she intends to continue her stellar performance. Miriam has a sales team but stays very involved in order to maintain her reputation. "There will be no dropping the ball; the process is clear."

LESSON LEARNED: Success is dependent on your relationship and communication. It leads to future referrals and more business.

SALES TIP: Good relationships require verbal communication. It is very important to talk with a client, not just send emails or texts.

ACTION PLAN: Build a good network for yourself. Announce your specialties. Build relationships with those you meet. Expand your client and prospect base. Plan your follow-through when the sale is made.

THE CLOSING PLAN

"Can you believe that most real estate agents do not even attend the closing of the house they just sold," Willie stated with disgust. They arrange to have their lawyer send them the commission check. Willie explained that this is the difference between a transactional salesperson and a relationship salesperson. The transactional salesperson does the basics of the job and has no interest in going beyond the basics or investing in their own self-development.

This bothered Willie so much that he designed his own "close plan." He knew this would benefit him and his agents. He wasn't sure just how much until he had a difficult sale on his hands.

Willie proceeded to tell his story. He had sold a moderate house to a nice couple years ago. He obviously did a good job because they called him when they were ready to upgrade to a larger home. What a great opportunity! He was to list their current home and help them buy a new one. He found them the perfect house. Sounds perfect, but not so fast—the people selling the larger home were in a nasty divorce, and the sale was not going to be smooth.

Willie met the couple buying the home in their soon-to-be new home for the final walk-through. The house had been left with bags of clothes in the living room, garbage in the kitchen, and a pile of keys on the counter. After some cleanup, they finally found a key or two that worked on the outside doors. They also found out that some neighbors might have had the duplicate keys. The new homeowners were not happy but were eager to get moved in.

Willie did not feel good about the whole problem with the house keys. He decided to call the new homeowner the next morning. He asked him how his first night in the new house turned out. The homeowner said it was an awful night. His wife could not sleep, thinking of who may have keys. She did not feel safe. Willie told the homeowner he would get back to him.

Willie could have called the old owners and dealt with some resistance, but instead he called his locksmith and had him go to the home and rekey every door. He also told the locksmith to bill him, not the new client. The homeowner was thrilled. Problem solved!

Willie did not stop there. This had been a valuable lesson. Willie decided it was time to create the closing plan. He knew that it was necessary to check in the day after the sale. He created a list of vendors he could use to solve any of the homeowner's problems or to provide good referrals to the new buyers.

Willie, thinking of the new buyers a month later, decided to check in with them again. They were so pleased with the attention received. The next day Willie got a call with a referral. And a month later, a call with another referral. And six months later, another referral. The close plan now includes calls scheduled for the day after the sale, thirty days later, six months later, and on the one-year anniversary of the closing. Since that time, Willie has added a study of the home's value to the one-year anniversary call. It may be time to move again!

"Relationship building is the key to being a successful real estate agent. It's the extras that will give you referrals and repeat business." This close plan led to more referrals and more listings and put Willie in the top three real estate agents in his area year after year from then on.

LESSON LEARNED: Your relationship with a client does not end with the sale.

SALES TIP: Strengthen your new relationships by going beyond the necessities to get repeat business and referrals.

ACTION PLAN: Prepare your own personal closing plan. Know what you should do after the sale is complete. Follow up and follow through.

DAY AFTER the sale: Action

30 DAYS after the sale: Action

6 MONTHS after the sale: Action

ONE-YEAR ANNIVERSARY of the sale: Action

CONTINUE PROVIDING VALUE

Vicki, a banking executive for many years, decided to focus on being a wealth advisor at the bank. She thought long and hard about the importance of networking, being involved in the community, and establishing some strong relationships with prospects. She talked about how important all of that was to her success but realized early on in her position that the "after-sale" may be more important to her long-term success.

Vicki talked about the excitement you feel when you close a new client. Some people celebrate and go on to work on another deal. Vicki learned that buyer's remorse is common. Often people will think about their decision and question whether or not they should have moved forward in the first place.

That is when the "after-sale plan" and relationship must begin. The customer needs to feel like they are part of your family now. They need to feel accepted and important. Vicki established a plan to strengthen the relationship right out of the gate. She welcomed the new client to the bank. She asked them how they would like to be serviced and what the relationship should look like. Vicki recommended to her clients to set up regular meetings with her, quarterly or biannually, depending on their comfort level. She explained to the client they would be reviewing a performance spreadsheet to keep an eye on all of their goals. She put the client on her newsletter email list so they could receive educational tips, market updates, and news. She invited the new client to a local event or a bank-sponsored event to get to know them a little more personally.

Vicki explained that as the comfort level solidifies and the client is comfortable with their choice, the relationship strengthens. As the relationship gets stronger, there is opportunity for upselling on additional products and services and securing a long-term client.

Vicki knew she was successful in the first year "after-sale" plan when a new client made a referral of a family member. Vicki's goal was to get a referral from all new clients within a year and hoped it would become an annual event.

LESSON LEARNED: Do not focus on making the sale only. Focus on providing continuous solutions with a strong relationship.

SALES TIP: "Swim in the deep end of the pool." Challenge yourself. Invest in self-development to be able to share value and solutions with your clients.

ACTION PLAN: Look at the big picture. How will you do what is best for the client after the initial sale? Think about your long-term relationships.

8

LOSING THE SALE

Develop an attitude of gratitude. Say thank you to every-
one you meet for everything they do for you.
—Brian Tracy

YOU CAN'T WIN THEM ALL

Ashtin worked for a technology company early in her
career. She was so focused on being successful right out
of the gate. She researched and prepared. She worked
hard on every proposal. She said, "You would think all of
that would earn me every new client. But that was not
the case." Ashtin was glad she learned a very valuable
lesson early in her career. This story has made her a
much better sales professional over the years.

Ashtin found a prospect who was ready to buy what

she had to offer. She was thrilled and was set to close this one quickly and make an impression on her new boss. She spent a great deal of time on the proposal. She delivered it, only to have the prospect ask for more at a lower rate. She added what he wanted, and he asked for more. In fact, when she followed up again, he asked again for a lower price. Ashtin pondered whether she should give the prospect what he wanted, but something didn't feel right. She decided to wait a week and call again in hopes she would get a different response. When she followed up, the prospect informed Ashtin that he had decided to give the business to a previous vendor who he had built a relationship and done business with in the past.

Ashtin reflected on this bad news. She felt used; her ego was crushed, and she took it hard. She said in retrospect it was a necessary lesson, and she would never forget this. The prospect was "playing" her so he could go back to his current vendor to negotiate. She realized that a strong sale leading to a long-term client must start with a relationship and honest discussions early in the process.

To this day Ashtin will never forget this. She has vowed to "interview" all her prospects and "select" the ones who fit. This lesson made her a very successful sales professional with confidence, honesty, and transparency.

LESSON LEARNED: Become particular about the prospects you want to work with. You do not need them all. Quality clients, not quantity.

> **SALES TIP:** Ask better questions. And if you have to ask if you are being "played," go right ahead and get the truth.
>
> **ACTION PLAN:** Be bold. Inquire. Be confident. It is best to be direct, honest, and transparent with people. Don't be afraid. It will pay off in the long term.

LEARN FROM YOUR MISTAKES

"After thirty years in sales, I have a lot of stories, but one story taught me a lesson I will never forget. And I think I need to share it with many people," said Anne.

"I had just graduated from college and taken my dream job in sales. My family always said I was perfect for sales. I had a great deal of success my first year working on straight commission. I had just bought my first new car. I was feeling a little cocky and thought I could do anything."

One morning Anne pulled into the parking lot of her first appointment just as a woman driving a beautiful Mercedes (much nicer than Anne's car) was pulling out and not looking behind her. Anne says, "No one was going to hit my new car! So I laid on my horn and gave her an unkind gesture. I felt badly afterward and knew it was the wrong thing to do, but it was too late. Oh, well. Time to go on with the day."

About a month later, Anne had scored a big appointment with the manager of a medical software company that had verified business. Anne was set on closing the account right away. The company needed the service, and it was going to be an easy sale. Not so fast...

As Anne entered the woman's office, she felt good and sat down. The manager turned to face Anne and discuss the business at hand. The conversation started out pretty well. But about five minutes later, the manager said to Anne, "I think we know each other." Anne denied ever meeting the manager but knew it was the woman she had had the nasty encounter with the month before. This was not good. Anne tried to keep the conversation going, but both parties knew this was not going to be good.

Obviously, the manager was done spending time with this cocky, young saleswoman who had previously told her off. She proceeded to end the meeting by asking for a proposal and said she would look it over. Anne knew this sale was not going to happen. And the manager never took Anne's call again.

Anne says in retrospect it may have been better to be honest with the woman. She said from that day forward she vowed to respect everyone and work on building a great reputation. As time went on, Anne built a solid reputation with her local network priorities and quickly landed among the top three salespeople in the Northeast.

LESSON LEARNED: It's a small world. People know each other. Etiquette matters. Honesty matters.

SALES TIP: Building your network within your community is very important. You want a good reputation.

BE PATIENT, AND WALK AWAY FROM A PROSPECT

When Eric was a young man, he had no idea what he wanted to do, so he started networking and applying for jobs that looked interesting. He had little education and little experience, but he said he was in the right place at the right time when he met his first "real" boss. Tim was a very successful commercial real estate broker and owner of his own company. He was not highly educated (in college) but put all his efforts into learning real estate and sales. Eric said Tim saw that Eric was much like he had been as a young man. Eric was offered the job. His boss told him he would train him, certify him, and be there to coach him to success. In turn, he expected Eric to listen to him and trust that he knew best.

Eric said he didn't always agree with Tim or like his style, but he trusted that he knew what he was doing due to all of the success he had gained over the years. The one lesson Eric learned was that he must follow up on all referrals and speak with potential prospects to assess whether they could work together. He also learned that sometimes you have to walk away from a deal if the deal is not going to work for both parties or the deal would not be successful in the end or the client does not appreciate the relationship.

Eric said one day he knew exactly what his boss meant by these lessons. Eric received a great lead to call a law firm that wanted to sell a ten-thousand-square-foot building and lease back only two thousand square feet for their use. He knew this could be a great deal—selling a building and negotiating a lease for the new owner. So Eric met with the managing partners of the firm that owned the building. Eric had done his home-work and explained what his research said and what a fair market price was for that market. Unfortunately, what Eric told the prospect was not what the prospect wanted to hear! The prospect became rude and told Eric he did not know what he was doing. Eric remained calm and respectful. He explained to the prospect that he wanted to be realistic and honest with them. Eric knew he had to walk away even though the deal had so much potential.

Eric, regretfully at first, recommended the sellers should interview other brokers and study the market-place. And Eric walked away from the deal.

A couple of days later, Eric received a call from that same prospect asking if they could meet again. The sellers apologized for their rudeness and told Eric they respected him and wanted to work with him. They met again, started a new conversation, made a deal, and sold the building, and everyone made money in the end. The deal was successful! And Eric learned to be patient and honest.

He also mentioned that the prospect does not always return. Sometimes they are not meant to be your client.

LESSON LEARNED: It's good to learn your own value and what your time is worth. The right people will respect you. Think about every potential deal and assess its worth.

SALES TIP: It is good to compete with confidence if you are patient and respectful. Do not be defensive.

ACTION PLAN: Ask your prospects a lot of questions. Why do they want to do that? What should the end result look like? And what are their expectations of you?

SOMETIMES YOU CAN SAVE A SINKING DEAL

Paul explained that he worked for an HR consulting firm specializing in outplacement services and talent development. He had been in sales for many years and felt he understood the fundamentals quite well. He knew he needed to ask questions, clarify the goals, and paint a picture of a successful end result.

Paul's company invested in a coaching application that allowed them to be very comprehensive in the sales process. It assisted with the information they needed and the great presentations they delivered. But one day there was a new lesson to be learned.

Paul and some of his colleagues had prepared a presentation, great questions, and even a tentative roadmap for closure. They knew their competition and were prepared to talk about the differences. They were meeting with a high-level VP of human resources—the decision-maker, of course. They were going to nail this one!

As the meetings went on, they built rapport, gave a good presentation, and planned to move into the closing stage. But something wasn't right. The VP of HR evaluated the two companies and started leaning toward the other company. She stopped giving them time and attention. The points she made were not factual. That did not seem to matter. As much as they continued to hear objections and address them, the deal looked like it would be lost.

Fortunately, they brought in one of their senior managers who knew the prospect's senior VP of human resources. Since they were at the end of their ropes, the senior-level person addressed the senior VP of HR. He explained that they felt they were losing in spite of everything that had been addressed. He asked for help understanding what may be missing and how they could remain in the process. The relationship the two gentlemen had was definitely a plus, but it was more than that. The sales team did not qualify the prospect's decision-making team. They assumed one person was the decision-maker. Other important players were left out of the process.

Paul explained that there are often "screeners" who gather information to bring back to their team. He went on to say that in order to be successful, all the players must be involved. It is up to the sales professional to qualify the decision-making team and the process.

When Paul and his sales group added the clarification of the decision-making process and the players and followed up with a clear roadmap, their sales went up. "It is important to cover the whole process and not rush to make a deal with missing information."

LESSON LEARNED: The questions you ask are the key to a successful deal. You must confirm their process and who the decision-makers are on a deal. Don't assume anything.

SALES TIP: It is fair to ask about multiple decision-makers. Most decisions are not made by one person but by a team or a committee.

ACTION PLAN: Be eager to ask the hard questions so you can understand the complete buying process. This allows you to lay out a roadmap or a project plan. This way everyone sees a timeline that leads to a successful endpoint. It makes everything clear, and it also makes it difficult to step out of a clear roadmap to success.

9

CULTIVATING REFERRALS

Networking is simply the cultivating of mutually benefi-cial, give and take, win-win relationships. It works best, however, when emphasizing the "give" part.
—Bob Burg

HOW DO I KEEP GETTING REFERRALS?

Cindy was a young banker just finishing up her train-ing program. The bank was looking to start a mortgage division. Cindy asked to be a part of the new division. Her experience level was minimal. She knew her target market was real estate agents and that she needed them to send her referrals. So the question was "How do I get the real estate agents to listen to me and send me refer-rals?" Why do they want to do business with me?

Cindy had minimal sales experience, but she did know that people buy from those they like. She thought she had a likeable personality, but that may not be enough to get continuous referrals—the key to her success. After giving this some thought, she decided to throw two educational sessions for the real estate agents: one at 8:00 a.m. and one at 4:00 p.m. She knew she should have food at these meetings to lure them in.

The food worked, and she had a good showing at both meetings. She secured some referrals and began building her database of real estate agents, referrals, and customers. She initially thought she was all set, but not so fast. Two weeks later she knew she had to make the connections a more regular part of her marketing efforts. Going forward, she planned regular educational meetings at 8:00 a.m. or at day's end. She began to build some solid relationships with the regulars who came in for breakfast or stopped on their way home from work. And she added a routine of calling everyone in her database on Fridays to say hello, thank them for the referrals, and wish them a great weekend.

Cindy's methodical sales plan was working, and she soon found herself the number one mortgage originator in the bank's New York State territory.

LESSON LEARNED: People need a reason to want to do business with you. Build a relationship.

SALES TIP: You must be visible to your target market to get repeat business and referrals.

FOCUSED REFERRAL SOURCES

When Tara started a new job selling cybersecurity, she researched top companies in her area and made some calls from these lists. She looked for requests for proposals (RFPs) that she could address. Tara also used LinkedIn to research potential contacts and alumni from her college who might have been willing to help her get appointments. All of these strategies worked to some extent, but what worked the best was a Partner Referral Plan.

Tara explained why this strategy was most effective in cultivating new business. These "partners" were companies in the same industry with the same target market but offered complementary services to their cyber product. Basically, the partners would share their contacts and relationships, which would lead to a shorter sales cycle. Both companies would have their own specialty, and the client really needed both of their products and services to accomplish the customer's desired outcome—a protected cybersecurity solution.

Who made a good partner, you ask? A company that has a good database of qualified prospects who have been screened and educated on what the market has to offer. The key to success was for Tara to continuously educate her partners—to give them the right information to offer to their clients. By the time she received the referral from the partner, they were sold on the service. Tara just had to close the deal, secure the relationship, and provide the details that were needed for each individual prospect.

Tara also learned that the relationship she built with partners was the key to her success. She needed to continue to provide valuable information that they could present to their clients. As the relationship strengthened, the referrals increased. When the trust was high, they often teamed up for appointments or for a joint proposal.

Tara knew this should be her strategy, especially when she closed her biggest clients to date from the partnership agreements that she had nurtured.

LESSON LEARNED: Don't stop selling until a "no" is forever. And don't step on the toes of your partners or referral sources. Cultivate trust.

SALES TIP: Always do what is best for the client. You are there to solve problems.

ACTION PLAN: Research potential alliances that complement your product or service to find qualified referral sources.

TALKING TO EVERYONE

Dan, a commercial real estate agent, told me he "lives and breathes from referrals." In his business, he needs to know what people are thinking about real estate about a year or two in advance. Dan said you can't just call a business owner and expect that person to immediately tell you that they are thinking of moving in a year. Most of the time, the prospect needs to meet you in person, build a relationship with you, and learn what options are out there. The relationship can be deep since the location of someone's business can depend on their growth and their goals. Because of this, Dan learned early on that he needed to let everyone know what he did for a living. His short elevator speech was important. And his visibility in his community was important. "You never know when you are going to get a referral. But you do know that if you provide value to someone, they just may want to thank you back."

Dan shared a story. One of the best referrals he ever received was from a neighbor. Dan noticed that his neighbor had not cleaned the snow from her driveway. Dan said she had recently moved in, and he wasn't sure she had family help or a snowblower. Dan went over and cleaned her driveway. The woman came out to thank him. And when she did, Dan told her his name and that he was a commercial real estate agent and was flexible if she needed anything. A few weeks later, the woman knocked on his door with a piece of paper. It was a referral—the name and business and contact information. She explained that she had met someone who wanted to move their office. Dan thanked her. Wow! When he followed up, he realized it was a great lead. He later closed a $2.4-million deal just because he had helped someone.

Dan also mentioned he has stayed involved in his community over the years. Visibility was important. He offered to give a class on negotiation skills for his local chamber of commerce. He said he knew he might be giving up a few hours to help others but that a lead just might come his way. An attendee of the class came right up to him after class with a lead.

Kindness and visibility have paid off for Dan!

LESSON LEARNED: You need to strive to be the best in your field by investing in your own self-development. And it's OK to share your knowledge with others.

SALES TIP: Tell people what you do for a living. A short elevator speech is enough. And invest time in your qualified leads. More will come from happy, satisfied people.

ACTION PLAN: Prepare your elevator speech. Also, make your own personal plan to cultivate leads, share knowledge, and be kind. Invest in yourself. Finding a great mentor is a plus.

BEING "PRESENT" INCREASES REFERRALS

Paula had been selling mortgages for almost thirty years. She explained what it was like in the early days. She joined clubs, went to networking events, and talked to everyone. She did not know where her next client would come from. Visibility was the key. As time went on, her "circle" grew, and referrals started coming in the door. She met the real estate community, her largest source of referrals. She took care of them. And she didn't have to market herself at every event like in the early days.

Paula learned that client service was very important to a successful transaction, repeat business in subsequent years, and referrals. Paula said she did a lot of "hand-holding," walking people through every step of the process. "I enabled them. They needed me," she explained and continued to talk about the rewards of taking care of everyone. This all worked, and her mortgage career became a huge success.

Reflecting back, she said she did almost everything right but sometimes neglected the sources of easy referrals. It took her many years and some embarrassment to realize that her closest friends and relatives didn't know what she did. Paula talked about being at a family event and hearing that her cousin had bought a house with a mortgage. When Paula asked who had written her mortgage, the cousin confessed she did not know Paula was a mortgage lender. She said that often sales professionals do not ask the people closest to them for help or referrals because "it's safer," just in case something goes wrong.

Feeling more confident after all these years, she talked about the importance of being visible and present. "It is OK to let everyone know what you do and to let them know you value referrals. Those that are comfortable with you will help." She makes sure to share that advice with others.

Although Paula will get an occasional message on Facebook asking where she is working now, most of her prior clients, referral sources, family, and friends know where she is. With her valuable contact management database and her networking skills, she remembers to encourage referrals. It sure has made new business much easier. "Referrals are more important than you realize!"

LESSON LEARNED: Some clients do not realize that you want the referrals, and they are important. Ask for referrals. Tell clients that "you are never too busy to help someone they know."

SALES TIP: Be more visible and top of mind with friends and family. Sometimes the people closest to you do not know what you do for a living. They will help.

ACTION PLAN: Use a contact management program to stay organized and follow up with prospects and clients.

TREAT EACH PERSON INDIVIDUALLY

Alissa has been a top financial planner in her industry for over thirty years. She started out as a young woman in a male-dominated industry. She spent most of her time networking in her community, giving educational seminars, and cultivating potential referrals. Early in her career, she surrounded herself with experienced professionals in the industry. When she captured an interested prospect, she consulted with specialists in her firm to bring a wide depth of expertise to benefit new professional relationships.

Over time, she found that the key to success was developing deep, meaningful relationships with clients by inquiring about each individual's needs, wants, and wishes. She probed to understand what had worked for them in the past and what had not worked. There was no "single" formula that could be applied to everyone. She knew she had to tailor solutions to each individual-ized need, whether they were single, a couple, a family, a small business, or a nonprofit. Every relationship was personalized with custom strategies.

When Alissa received a referral or made a contact, she knew she had to follow her proven strategy—first ask questions and listen, then build a relationship, follow a process to service them, and ask for referrals when you do your job well.

If that sounds easy, think again. She was in a very crowded field. She needed to set herself apart from others. Alissa would offer a "second opinion" to those who said they were happy with their current service. She focused on seeing how she could add additional or unique value to what they were currently doing. It was important to provide "extras"—information that helped people with their whole lives, with an "advice beyond investing" approach. These extras have varied over the years, including connections to tax and estate planning professionals, long-term care planning and assisted living options, philanthropy strategies, social impact investment resources, and small business advanced planning insights, lending solutions, cybersecurity tools, and more.

Alissa attributed her long career successes to responding on an individual basis, building trust, and bringing each person information and resources to contribute to their needs, wants, and wishes. Doing the right thing and offering the "extras" have contributed to her referrals over the years. She knew that a referral meant she had earned a client's trust and provided customized solutions, and they wanted others to have the same great experience they had.

Alissa's referrals have been consistent over the years due to years of hard work and genuinely caring about her clients. She has been in the business for thirty years, and it is important for her to receive these great referrals from one generation to the next. Alissa remained on top by taking interest in each person individually and finding the resources that added quality to each person's lifestyles.

LESSON LEARNED: "People don't care how much you know until they know how much you care."

SALES TIP: Listen to what people want and need, and tailor to each person individually.

ACTION PLAN: Write a personal business plan that includes relevant statistics, services, target markets, strategy, and focus—a guide for what to do to succeed. Review and update quarterly.

10

ENSURING REPEAT BUSINESS AND CLIENT RETENTION

Sell your merchandise at a reasonable profit, treat your customers like human beings, and they will always come back for more.
—L. L. Bean

BE A PARTNER, NOT JUST ANOTHER VENDOR

Art, a commercial banker, explained that most banks have the same products and services these days, so it is very important to differentiate yourself from other bankers. "A banker needs a style to set himself apart from others, and I had to think about what type of banker I wanted to be." He went on to say that he really disliked pushy salespeople who talk too much. It was very important to him to not be that person. He went on to explain that he is straightforward and "real," someone who people can relate to honestly. Art called his style one of "conversational transactions." The conversation flows naturally, and often an opportunity surfaces.

Art's clients consisted primarily of real estate developers, entrepreneurs, and business owners. All of them started out small, a loan or two. He established relationships with all of them, getting to know their businesses and their goals. "In order to retain a client and ensure repeat business, they have to like and trust you. It's only at that time the client will listen to you as you cross-sell them or educate them on other products and services you offer. And it's important to *not* push a product that simply does not make sense for them."

Art designed a personal retention plan for each individual client. Some clients liked a quarterly visit, and some preferred an annual check-in. Either way, being responsive to the customer's expectations is vital to success.

Art reviewed all of his relationships on a regular basis, learned about each client individually, and watched his clients grow over time. He mentioned that, over the past ten years, his small clients have gotten larger. He saw success as the range of new loans increased. He realized that if you stick with your client and understand them personally, retention becomes so much easier.

One of Art's clients, an area real estate developer, told him that he felt like Art was part of his business, not just another pushy salesperson. The developer grew, and the banking business followed suit.

LESSON LEARNED: Be genuine and interested in the people you meet. People like to talk about themselves!

SALES TIP: Manage expectations from the start—under-promise and overdeliver.

ACTION PLAN: Learn what the client wants and needs so your cross-selling and retention are successful. Share information as an educator in a casual conversation. Do not push products and services that are not needed or wanted.

THE WALLS HAVE EARS

Vicki started her career in the healthcare insurance industry by accident. She originally started with a career in retail and moved to a nice management position quickly. A shopper liked Vicki's communication style and asked her to apply for a claims processing position with the potential to move up quickly. Vicki applied, uneducated in this industry but looking for a change in position with better hours.

Vicki was fortunate to get her first new position in claims processing, with a fabulous boss. Her boss always had great advice. He said, "The walls have ears; remember to protect your image and always do the right thing." Vicki took this advice to heart. She was conscious of her image, worked toward building great relationships, and communicated positively. Obviously, this worked for her. She moved from claims processing to a customer service position. She continued to be noticed for her great people skills, and her boss "pushed" her into a sales position.

Vicki did not have a sales background or any sales training. But she knew how to treat people well and how to be a true professional. When her company was having a problem selling benefits to the chambers of commerce in the region, they assigned Vicki this challenging task. Vicki quickly established relationships with each chamber's staff, insurance brokers, and some hospital affiliates. She was responsible for selling and maintaining these accounts. Client retention and repeat renewals were so important and so were the long-term relationships she built along the way.

Vicki was so successful that she closed all twenty-four chamber of commerce locations, added additional products, and exceeded 100 percent of goal year after year. Vicki attributed her success to selling the right products to the right people—selling what works for each client.

The relationships she built over many years did not go away. When Vicki decided to start her own company selling Medicaid insurance, she reached out to her old clients and contacts and landed new opportunities with many of the same people. She attributed her "client retention" to upholding her reputation, treating people well, and cultivating relationships over many years.

LESSON LEARNED: Always do the right thing! Sell products and services only if it is a fit for both parties.

SALES TIP: Be upbeat. Your goal is to help people. Find something that you believe in and that you know is helpful to others. Spread your passion.

ACTION PLAN: Stay busy. Alternate your activities between new and existing business. Spend time prospecting, spend time reaching out to referrals, and spend time on customer service and retention. Send a useful mailing and then follow up. Consider offering educational seminars to educate clients and prospects.

ACTIVITY CREATES OPPORTUNITY

Larry explained you must learn a great deal about the staffing business to be successful in it. He mentioned there are two types of strategies—one is a blended desk strategy, where one person is the recruiter and the salesperson. The other type of organization has a recruiter who specializes in the operations side and a salesperson who specializes in the sales side. The recruiter is the farmer who goes and gets the right candidates for the positions. The salesperson is the hunter who goes and gets the job orders. The salesperson establishes the relationship with the key decision-maker. The recruiter builds the relationship with the hiring manager. Both positions are involved with ensuring repeat business and retention by making the clients happy.

The recruiter often hears from the hiring manager that a new position is being added. And the salesperson makes sure that the decision-maker gets the results he needs to run a successful business.

Larry talked about his sales strategy and the process that has delivered success to him and his team over the years. He explained the "20 Zone Planner," in which a territory is broken into 5 zones and subdivided into 4 additional zones. This strategy allowed him to focus on one area at a time rather than driving or calling in a large territory. This increased productivity and focus. Each calendar work day (around twenty days), he would visit clients and prospects in one area of the zone. This increased face time with clients and made it easy to tell the client the next time he would be in the area in order to schedule an appointment. More face time often led to repeat business and helped to keep the competition out. Visibility was his key to success.

In addition to seeing regular clients on a schedule, the 20 Zone Planner allowed him to call prospects for meetings in each territory. "It was easy to say that I would be in their area on a certain day, visiting x client nearby," explained Larry.

After many years in the staffing industry working under different processes, Larry settled in on a disciplined sales process using the 20 Zone Planner that has worked for him for many years now. His goal is to acquire and retain clients for many years. That is what has increased his revenue and success over the years.

LESSONS LEARNED: Stay away from making pricing your key issue. It is rarely the real issue. People want a quality product or service with great customer service. Sales is a process, so don't rush it.

SALES TIP: Ask a lot of questions. And it is OK to answer a question with another question. Yes and no are great answers that can be addressed. The worst response you can hear is maybe. Keep asking questions to avoid a maybe.

ACTION PLAN: Study your territory. Identify and research all of the companies in your area. Make phone calls. Clarify prospects, and work the territory. Have a plan.

MY REPUTATION IS KEY

Jim, the key sales representative for a hundred-year-old construction company, explained that he went to work there because it had a very good, longstanding reputation. He said, "I needed to believe in the company to uphold my own reputation." Jim went on to talk about his target market of architects, engineers, colleges, hospitals, and schools. They were all in it for the long term. There would be more than one project, so you never wanted to "burn bridges." To be successful, he had to focus on client retention for repeat business and additional projects over the years.

Jim set up an annual retention plan. He said it was nothing fancy but included calls and visits. He would seek out valuable information about the marketplace, materials, or local opportunities. He would share this information with his client base. His goal was to be creative and find them opportunities such as land for development, specific rehab opportunities, and buildings and lots in the right areas. The clients would seek him out early in their planning for information on construction and everything that goes with it. Jim acted as a "project consultant" to his closest clients.

He had to check his "core values" when a project seemed too good to be true. Jim told me a customer called him with a big job that seemed to be a good opportunity. The client knew how he wanted to proceed. Jim said he saw a flaw and tried to educate the client on other options. The client did not want to hear about other options. Jim said he knew the project was not going to be successful. He turned it down to save his relationship and values in hopes of a future opportunity. It was not worth killing a relationship. The client did call him in when the project hit a stumbling block and told Jim he understood why he had tried to stop him. The client returned with a new project a year later. The relationship was rekindled, and Jim held his reputation.

LESSON LEARNED: Never take a shortcut. Be thorough. Tell the truth even if it means you have to turn the business down.

> **SALES TIP:** Be honest. Integrity is so important. Be knowledgeable about your profession. Research everything ahead of appointments, but listen first and then provide value.
>
> **ACTION PLAN:** Think about the long term, and build lasting relationships. Create opportunities for your clients to guarantee more business.

PROVIDE GREAT EXPERIENCES

Laura had been in the hotel and hospitality industry for many years. She explained that this was a competitive industry. "If you don't service your customer, someone else will."

Her job seemed to look easy to some people. Laura was out meeting people at great events, socializing on many evenings, and making some great connections. This routine was not all for fun. Laura learned that she needed a lot of connections to strike a lead. And once she got the lead, a contract had to be secured and many details needed to be worked out.

Laura went on to say that like many sales professionals, she has learned many lessons over the years. She attributed her success to a few key practices:

- Listen and grasp every detail.
- Deliver what you promised, and follow up to secure more business.

- When the event guests are impressed, you have earned new prospects.
- Great experiences bring people back.

After years hunting business, Laura leads a small team. She is still selling and sharing her advice with coworkers and her team. The group's focus is to expand their contacts, deliver a great experience, and follow up to ensure more business. The key is that repeat business is easier and less expensive than new business. Once you set up client details, along with building a secure relationship, the rest is in the details. Fortunately, she has had annual events that are often similar from year to year. "It's so important to provide the best experience you can for every event. You need a new client to return in order to increase your revenues year after year." Fortunately, Laura's business grew over time. She explained that following her list of best practices led to the right results.

LESSON LEARNED: Deliver what you sell. Be trustworthy, authentic, and honest. Listen.

SALES TIP: Repeat business is less expensive than new business.

ACTION PLAN: You need the tools to succeed, and that means you need to meet many people. Help your connections succeed, and they will return the favor. Show a sincere interest in others' success.

11

UPSELLING AND CROSS-SELLING

Here is a simple but powerful rule—always give people more than they expect to get.
—Nelson Boswell

A "HUG" AND SOME EDUCATION FOR MORE BUSINESS

Pam spent many years in the insurance industry. She strongly believed her success was attributed to the strong relationships she built over the years. Pam explained, "You need to get close to your clients. It's much harder to say no or to get rid of your vendor after a hug." Pam went on to say that her relationship building was built not only on her interest in them but on her ability to educate her clients on topics of interest, industry information, or competitive information. Pam's company sent out a client newsletter for many years filled with educational information. Pam did not rely solely on the client reading the newsletter; she highlighted specific information that pertained to them. Pam focused on products and services that she thought her client needed in addition to what they already had. She believed a soft sell approach, a handwritten note, or an email highlighting information was a successful tactic to grow sales in her existing client base. Her goal was to be known as a consultant or an advisor, not just a salesperson.

Over the years, Pam was recognized as an educator of her clients. They learned to trust her and bought more products and services from her. Her cross-selling and upselling increased year after year. She earned a partnership in her agency from her strong performance over the years. And Pam reminded us all that "more revenue means more commission and a stronger client relationship."

LESSON LEARNED: If you move too slowly, you lose opportunities—move too fast, and you scare them away.

SALES TIP: People buy from who they like and trust. Success will come when you build a strong relationship.

ACTION PLAN: Show your clients you are knowledgeable by educating them and ensuring you are there to help them. Educate your clients by sharing valuable and useful information.

FOLLOW A SALES PROCESS

Dawn was a trained psychologist when she met her future husband, a sales professional. Her husband decided to open his own business, and she decided to join him in building a successful business selling fax machines, copy machines, and other office equipment.

Dawn knew little or nothing about sales. She started calling people and asking questions. She learned what her prospects wanted and saw some early success. As the business grew, she realized she needed a team. Her psychology background helped her choose a successful sales team. She learned quickly that not everyone knew what to do on a daily basis. The key was to follow a sales process. "If the process was clear, their team would achieve success. And with the industry and technology changing, it was obvious that upselling and cross-selling were ways to add more revenue quickly." Dawn went on to say that you want your client list to grow so you can go back and sell new products and services. New clients take more time to cultivate than the existing clients you have built a relationship with. A good sales process reminds you to sell more to your client base.

It is obvious that even good sales professionals need direction. They need to follow a process. Dawn went on to say that she used to tell new salespeople to shadow the successful people, and they would be all set. But that was not enough for most new people. The team learned that if they had a process and a daily plan, they would remain focused on growth.

Since the upselling and cross-selling were so important to their business, they established a process that included email campaigns, follow-up, and regular scheduled visits to all clients. When someone became a client, they automatically scheduled two to three visits for the rest of that year. This would leave the door open to review needs, educate the clients on new products, and keep the relationship strong. A comprehensive customer database was developed that alerted the salespeople to the customer's expired contracts, upcoming visits, and outdated equipment. The sales team knew exactly what they needed to do every day and whom they should contact.

Their small team expanded, revenue grew, and the client retention rates kept increasing. After more than thirty years in business, they can report that many of their original clients are still with them today, and many of them are second-generation contacts. The sales process kept them disciplined and focused for many years, and the results followed.

LESSON LEARNED: The best sales professionals need to know about best practices and to have a roadmap that leads to success.

SALES TIP: Relationships are more important than you think. Before you stop in for a visit, prepare a conversation. It's worth checking LinkedIn contacts to see whom you both know. It keeps your relationship strong.

> **ACTION PLAN:** Follow a daily plan outlining calls, emails, appointments, and follow-up. With a daily list, you will stay focused.

USING A CREATIVE VALUE STRATEGY

Kelly explained to me that she had been selling newspaper advertising for over twenty-five years. The industry had changed drastically and almost was dissolved when digital and social media became the popular solutions over traditional print. She went on to say that she considered switching industries out of fear of losing everything she had built over the years. Kelly had a large list of clients and prospects and spent a great deal of time building relationships, but that was no longer enough.

The alarm sounded when she started hearing people say they were no longer interested in newspaper ads. There were other ways for them to attract business. That is when she knew she needed to learn more about her own industry trends and the trends in the overall marketplace.

Kelly started educating herself—reading, looking toward big markets for new ideas, and asking her clients what they were interested in. She brought her research to the newspaper management team. She recommended education, market research, digital options, social media, and event targeting. She called her new style a value strategy that was a creative bundling of many services (print, digital, online, and event targeting).

Kelly spent hours learning how her industry was changing and finding experts so she could learn even more. Eventually, her employer hired experts so she could bring them out on calls to help educate her clients. Not only did she have a reason to see everyone, but she also brought industry news, new options, and experts to help educate her clients. The old advertising strategy transformed into a comprehensive marketing and visibility strategy.

Kelly found her sales increasing. And her clients were thrilled to see her and learn about all of the new tools available to them. She could upsell her loyal, large base of clients with updated services. The new options afforded her revenue growth and stability in her position. She remained at the top of the producer's list.

LESSON LEARNED: You must invest in continuous learning and be open to change. Your contacts expect new ideas and solutions.

SALES TIP: Do not forget to service your clients. They need attention. Continuously ask questions and find solutions that make their business stronger.

ACTION PLAN: Figure out the right target market for you. Study that market, and know what will sell. Educate yourself, and share your knowledge with your prospects and clients.

INVESTIGATE THE BUYING PROCESS BY ASKING QUESTIONS

Joe had been selling transportation software for many years. He said he learned so much in the early days by just asking many questions. It didn't dawn on him until years later that the key to successful sales were the questions he continuously asked his clients and prospects.

Joe continued to explain that there are two types of prospects: the buyer who knows what they want versus the buyer who needs an education. Either way, one must ask so many questions to figure out what to sell them, how much to sell them, whom to sell to, and why they will buy. The buying process is like a puzzle that you need to put together. You need the influencer, the buyer, and the decision-maker to agree on many things if the deal is going to happen. Highly unlikely all the players will agree, Joe reiterated, because if they did, we would be able to sell them everything all at once.

What Joe learned was that sometimes you find all the parties agree on one part of the deal. That is when it is a good strategy to sell a piece of your solution and gain the new client's trust before upselling or cross-selling on other products and services. This strategy became so important to Joe that he trained his entire team on this new sales process. It started with painting a great vision of having all of the software products and services but offering a trial on a small piece of the solution. For example, a small school district could never afford the software. Joe worked with his team on "stepping stones"—buying the first stone and adding to the path later on. It became very important to the upsell and cross-sell process to add "account reviews" scheduled throughout the year or years. Basically, during an account review, a great representative would ask the client, "What are you using now? What do you need for the future?" The account executive might say, "I see you are using products one and two but not three and four." And the customer thinks you are trying to sell him number five, but since that is not the case, the account executive goes on to offer to remove products three and four after explaining the sales process "journey." Joe said that what actually happened was the customer liked your honesty, you gained some trust, and they opened up to becoming more interested in the whole solution. Over time, the customer saw the value, and the cross-sell or upsell was successful.

Using this strategy and sales process, and adding more great questions, allowed Joe to break into a smaller market and increase their product offerings over time. In addition, account executives were added to the team, and they focused on upselling and cross-selling the small clients and offering additional products and services to existing larger clients.

LESSON LEARNED: Know the profile of the right customer for you. And figure out the way to make them happy. Be their "solutions partner."

SALES TIP: Ask many, many questions! If the prospect is not interested, ask, "What would have to happen for you to talk with me?"

ACTION PLAN: Know all the players involved in the sales process (influencer, buyers, and decision-makers). Learn what motivates them to move forward, and learn what keeps them up at night.

12

VALUE SELLING

Price is what you pay. Value is what you get.
—Warren Buffet

LOOK AT THE BIG PICTURE

Kim went to college for social work and landed a job with a center for the disabled. She enjoyed her job but wanted to help more. She realized that advocating for the disabled would provide more value if she were an attorney. So Kim went off to law school to be an elder law attorney. Kim was focused on learning as much as she could in order to help families with their comprehensive needs, not just the basic law.

Kim set out to be an expert and to learn as much as she could about helping the disabled, including the funding, the politics, and the agencies available to help those in need. It wasn't just about the law. It was about consulting with the families on services and funding that were available, including assisted living services. When a family comes for legal help in this field, they need to see the big picture and everything that is involved, and Kim set out to learn everything.

She attended conferences on different services and how the law fit in. Her goal was to be a valued asset to the family. When they needed to understand services and funding and agencies and extended care, they could count on Kim. The families felt comfortable confiding in Kim and open to discussing many issues in their lives. Her legal costs became less of a discussion during her consultations. The clients saw the value she brought and built strong relationships with her.

Over time, Kim became known as the legal expert in elder law and the disabled. The referrals increased. The legal revenues increased, and she was promoted to a senior counsel position.

LESSON LEARNED: You can't just focus on doing your job; you need to invest time into self-development and educating yourself. You need to ask a lot of questions, attend educational conferences, and read updates in your field if you want to be a continued success.

SALES TIP: Find an agency or a cause that is meaningful to you, and get involved so you can become immersed in your field or your community. Continuous learning is important if you want to be an expert in your field. People buy from those they trust.

DO YOU REALLY NEED TO OFFER A DISCOUNT?

Don had been selling medical software for a few years. He knew the software had value. It would help so many organizations function more effectively. The days of running a doctor's office with "old tools" or "piecemeal" systems were over.

Don really liked to meet with the practice management managers that saw the value in his software. He knew it was a major expense but also knew the rewards were big, and the payback was relatively quick.

One day Don had an opportunity to meet with a hospital that had just made a major acquisition and needed to put one system in place and combine all the locations into one easy-to-use system. He knew he had the solution to their problem. His boss was thrilled to hear about the opportunity and the big-ticket potential. Don's boss asked to accompany Don to the appointment with the top dealmaker.

On the way to the appointment, Don saw his boss making calculations. He seemed to have quite a bit of stress on his face. Don calmly asked what was wrong. His boss explained that he was working on the discount levels they might have been able to offer the hospital. He really wanted to close this very large deal. Don knew that a discount might not have been necessary since the need was quite apparent and the timing was perfect.

Don asked his boss a few questions, in a role reversal from the norm. Don asked him to explain why they needed the software and how fast they wanted the implementation. When his boss answered the simple questions concerning value, it was clear that they needed to slow down and assess the situation. Don laid out the scenario—the hospital had just made a $25-million dollar acquisition. The new locations had to be integrated together in a very short span of time. Installations would be a priority to their offices. And all that solved with the ticket price of $2.6 million, far less than the merger price! And they could put a rush on the implementation.

Don politely asked his boss to let him close the deal on value selling, not price. Don asked the "value" questions, proceeded to lay out the scenario for the perfect implementation, and offered a successful solution. The prospect never asked the price until the deal was closed. No discount needed. Sale was successful!

LESSON LEARNED: If you ask the right questions, you will know the customer's true needs and the value they place on the products or service.

SALES TIP: Don't rush to close. Understand the value that the customer sees.

IT'S NOT ALWAYS ABOUT PRICE

Karen got a great job with the leader in legal services, LexisNexis. She quickly moved up to the position of top person in her region. Karen enjoyed working for the "best" in the industry. She had a strong brand that everyone knew. Price was not really a factor in her sales. She was selling the company's reputation, size, and strength in its market. All she had to do was build a relationship with the clients and prospects in her area.

A few years into the job, things changed. A new competitor came into her region. And the number two was looking to cause her some grief. Not only did the company have great services to offer at a lower price, but they also hired a superstar salesperson in her territory. The heat was on. Karen felt some of her business chipping away. It was time to reevaluate her options to stay number one. She was motivated to review everything when she lost out on a big trip (by less than $2,000!) awarded to top performers.

The first thing Karen did was call the competitor's salesperson for a meeting. She should know her competition, right? She was very disappointed to find out he was a nice guy, and he was hungry. Her first crazy thought—what would it be like if he were no longer in that position? Karen said her second crazy thought was giving his name to every recruiter who called her. It might have been a good idea, but it wasn't going to be enough.

It was time to reevaluate value selling. It's not just about price. Karen explained, "I wrote down all of the great reasons we had so many customers and were at the top in the industry. I pondered what was important to the customer—customer service, technology, security, strong brand, and personalized service from me." Karen really changed her selling style to focus on all of the extras she offered. She talked about service. She provided a number directly to her for emergencies. She educated her clients on all of the new products and technology. And the result—Karen became number one again and a far better salesperson. She said, "It's really amazing how good you can be when you have someone nipping at your tail."

LESSON LEARNED: Elimination of your competitors is not always possible, nor does it always work. You need to focus on your own selling skills.

SALES TIP: Sell your brand and your service, not just price.

ACTION PLAN: Write down all the value you can provide to a client—tangible and intangible. And figure out how to incorporate your assets into your selling process. Try educating.

BUSINESS DEVELOPMENT IS MORE THAN A SIMPLE SALE

Lisa, now a partner in a prominent local accounting firm, learned early on that accounting wasn't just about numbers. Providing financial statements alone did not offer the value the clients were seeking. She knew the relationship needed to be deeper than that. It was important to bond with people you met at a networking event, a community event, or on a board. You needed to "connect," find a common thread, an interest, or a topic for discussion outside of regular business.

When the COVID-19 pandemic hit the United States and everyone "shut down," Lisa knew how important the relationships she built really were. And she knew it was time to help her clients and her network to sort through their pain and get help. Businesses were looking to do anything to survive and keep going under some rough guidelines. Lisa said, "People wanted to know what financial aid was out there, how they were going to keep their employees, and what were they going to do in the short term that provided hope for the future." This pain and ignorance created an opportunity for her and her firm to brand themselves as experts—consultants, advisors, and educators.

It was important to make that first call basically asking how everyone was doing and what was on their minds. This allowed her to strengthen her client bond; to show human compassion and understanding. "People were scared and confused. They wanted to talk and to hear that someone cared to help them. I wanted to help them. And be known as their partner, not just a number cruncher."

Lisa explained that she and her partners immediately got together and developed educational information. They learned quickly the importance of virtual presentations and online meetings. They spoke about loans and financial assistance, but they went so much further to learn about the person's business, their goals, and what results they were trying to achieve.

Being out front and addressing the crisis resulted in full client retention, interested prospects, and many happy people who were part of their network of referral sources. She realized that she and her partners could "shine" during the worst of times as long as they focused on helping people and solving problems.

LESSON LEARNED: Even accountants need to sell their services to be successful. And they must understand that it takes patience to get through a long sales cycle. Building strong relationships is the key.

SALES TIP: It's all about relationships that you build in your network. You need to be visible, join the right groups, take the right board seats, and spend your time listening, inquiring, and educating. If you expect to receive referrals, you need to give value in return.

ACTION PLAN: Focus on business development early on in your career. Find a good mentor to help you select groups to get involved with. These groups become your circle of influence, your referral base, and your sounding board. Develop these relationships. When they are strong, invest in another group to expand your circle of influence.

SOLVE PROBLEMS

Jon and his partner, Mike, started a custom software development company in the early 2000s. It seemed to be a great match. Jon specialized in the technical end and did much of the office work. Mike focused on sales and growing the business. He was often seen networking in the community and calling people on the phone to solicit business. The company grew, and they were up to around ten employees by 2010. But the unexpected happened: Mike was offered a position by a big client of the company, and he accepted! Jon was left alone to run the company and provide work and revenue that would pay his team. Jon felt he knew nothing about sales. But quite to the contrary...

Jon thought long and hard about why someone would want to do business with him. Why didn't these prospects just buy off-the-shelf software? Often it was cheaper and came with plenty of support options. He began to look at his client base and the projects they had done over the years. There were a few very good reasons why people wanted to do business with them. Jon realized that sales was not just presenting the service and closing the deal. It was so important to provide real value to the client. His clients wanted ideas and "tools" that would improve their businesses and set them apart from the competitors.

Jon knew his job was to ask many questions to the C-suite of any prospect. He had to learn about their industry, their goals, and the current economic conditions. It was Jon's job to provide new ideas and solve problems for their clients and prospects. He needed to set them apart from their competitors and help each one succeed. That made the price less relevant to the deciding factors in selecting software. It was all about the value he brought them. It was about the solutions he could provide them to get ahead and be different.

Jon mentioned a great example. He met with the top management of a family-owned pool company that had been around for some time. This generation was looking to grow the company and expand nationally and beyond. The management team explained the problems they were having with ordering, providing prompt customer service, and billing and shipping parts and equipment. After Jon asked many questions, he asked them if state-of-the-art integrated technology that made order taking, shipping, and delivery simple could give them the growth they desired. This process and this technology could be the key for the needed improvement. That was the value proposition. Jon submitted the proposal, closed a new client, and helped them double their business in a short span of time. And as a bonus, Jon became quite involved in learning different aspects of their business and continued to add value by doing additional projects for them for many years.

The result was perfect—the company kept growing rapidly. It became an industry leader. The company's value and revenue increased, and eventually the company was sold for a big return to the owners. "Value sells!"

LESSON LEARNED: You need to continue to add value and invest in a relationship. Provide ideas without giving all the resources for the client to do it themselves.

SALES TIP: Know your value. Sell your value. Price is less important if the results are apparent.

ACTION PLAN: Learn your customer's business, industry, and their competitors. Provide them a valuable solution that sets them above the rest of their industry.

SELLING BIG—KNOW THE VALUE OF YOUR COMMUNITY

Most of Gina's career centered on tourism and economic development. She explained the importance of seeing the big picture and integrating yourself in your community. "My jobs have always been about selling a region or a community, not just a product or service."

Gina began her career working for a mall owner.

Gina's job was to enhance the experience for everyone at the mall—the tenants, the customers, the food court, and even maintenance. And the company paid everyone on the sales of the whole mall. This taught all the mall stakeholders the importance of providing the perfect overall experience to their customers. Gina explained that this job taught her so much about the importance of selling the vision, value, and the big picture. It taught her about "community."

These lessons proved to be valuable in Gina's next position, bringing visitors to a small city outside a true tourist area. Gina explained that her focus was to "put heads in beds." But it was much more than that. She needed to meet everyone in the community who was involved in tourism and events. If people were going to get a hotel room, it would mean they needed a reason to come here. She learned to work with corporations holding conferences, sporting event planners, performers, and many others who were involved in bringing revenue into the community. Gina knew she was doing the right thing when she saw the event calendar increasing and the hotel occupancy fees increasing. And she continued to emphasize the need to work with all her "partners" that made "things happen."

Gina said her most recent position focused more on individuals than corporate events. Even though tourism and destination events are her new focus, the community still plays a major role in her success. Gina took all her background experience, relationship skills, and community knowledge and put it to use building her next career.

Gina said her focus on providing value to the whole community has contributed to her success. Gina encouraged sales professionals to focus more on value, regardless of their specific product or service. Salespeople need to know that they are problem solvers. "If you can't solve their problem or provide them value, you need to know who can!"

LESSON LEARNED: "Sales" is personal! In the case of small businesses and family businesses, it is so important to build personal relationships. People buy from those they like and trust. And people will call you for the resources they need. Help everyone and treat them well, and they will be a long-term contact or client.

SALES TIP: Be a resource to everyone. Give referrals to help your contact base. These referrals will reward you with return referrals.

ACTION PLAN: Know what you are selling, who is involved, and what makes them happy. Investigate your community so you can help your clients with complementary services in your area. Think big!

Conclusion

LET ME TELL YOU ABOUT SUCCESS

For the past ten months, I have been fortunate to speak with so many great sales performers. I contacted past employees, people who have attended my training classes, people I have coached, and even some great friends who are true sales professionals. I think the thing that amazed me the most was their willingness to share stories, experiences, and sales tips with so much candor. No one seemed to feel like they had to hide anything. Some of the stories were just a little over the top, and maybe some of them I should have left out. I decided it was important to see "good" stories and even a few success stories that were not perfect. Everyone enjoys an honest person.

As I reflected on my long career working with many salespeople in many different industries, I found many common traits that successful people shared. The three that stood out most were *problem solver, personality with humor, and a sincere interest in helping others.* The most successful people can talk to anyone. They genuinely like others. I put together a full checklist to help managers, recruiters, and leaders.

CHARACTERISTICS OF TOP SALES PERFORMERS

- They ask questions.
- They build relationships.
- They are creative throughout the sales process.
- They have strong networks.
- They provide value with solutions.
- They learn from others.
- They have character and a good work ethic.
- They have empathy when needed.
- They are often a "personal brand."
- They are resilient, can see vision, and can adjust.
- They seek opportunity.

SHARING THEIR ADVICE

My favorite part of the interview process has been hearing the professionals' sales tips and the lessons they have learned along the way. I observed that most people had a love for storytelling. They could paint a picture of an experience, talk about what was right and wrong, and share the changes they would have made. Each one of them seemed grateful to have walked away with an experience they could reflect on down the road.

I remember learning so much from other salespeople in my early days. It was like every sales representative was some type of mentor. When they were telling a memorable story, they automatically talked about what they would have done differently. The lessons they had learned were very apparent. The sales tips these great professionals shared were priceless, especially for a rookie in the field. The three sales tips that stood out in my mind were:

- Build a network for learning, sharing ideas, support, and referrals.
- Know what value you offer. Use that to solve problems and create opportunities.
- Your most important skill is learning to ask questions and listening to the answer.

TIPS FOR SALESPEOPLE

- Love your job.
- Love people.
- Love to solve problems.
- Love to create opportunity.

- See forward.
- Be visible.
- Take interest.
- Listen.

TIPS FOR SALES MANAGEMENT

- Invest in the best. They will get better.
- Support, but don't micromanage.
- Encourage self-development.
- Set clear goals. Manage by expectations.
- Make training an interactive experience.
- Educate your team so they are prepared for the future.
- Make your evaluations a two-way discussion.

TIPS FOR SALES RECRUITERS

- Be sure your candidate tells you a story or two.
- Make sure you ask about their worst day or a lost sale.
- Ask for at least three lessons they have learned along the way.
- Ask what or who has influenced their success.
- Get the advice they offer to others in the field.
- Have a conversation. Test their communication skills and interest in others.

THOUGHTS FROM SUCCESSFUL SALES LEADERS

Along the way, I have met many sales managers and sales leaders. Managers spend too much time managing their team with criticism and a "to-do" list. Sales leaders motivate, strengthen their team, and offer support that leads to success. A true leader can help someone excel beyond their own expectations. And sometimes a typical sales manager can crush the spirit of a great sales professional.

These great sales leaders are not all the same. They may lead and manage very differently, and all these different styles can still lead to success. It is worth reviewing sales management styles emphasized in the success stories in this book. Many people interviewed commented on their managers.

Let me share a few stories to reflect on sales leadership styles.

Process. Dan is employed by a leader in CRM (customer relationship management) solutions. He said it's simple: sales are predictable when you have a goal, an understanding of the customer, and a roadmap to get there. Dan explained that you must manage your opportunities through a process. And the data you collect during that process must be documented. You can easily pick up where you left off. The sales team will get comfortable following the same path with each client. Dan talked about asking questions, listening, and understanding your customer and then figuring out how you are going to help the client. Once you make a plan, you can simply follow the process to success. When the data is documented, you can walk the client or prospect through your vision to the end result. "Giving the sales team what they need from start to finish ensures that nothing is left out. When a representative is clear on value proposition, they can get creative, tell a story, or paint a vision so the roadmap to success is very clear."

Support. Dawn, a psychologist by training, found herself a business owner and a sales manager. She explained that she thought she was good at hiring the right sales representatives most of the time but didn't think she should leave them to be self-directed. "I believe that management needs to provide some guidance and support to their revenue producers to increase their success. I give them a roadmap to follow, a daily plan, set them up with good technology to manage clients, prospects, and to-do lists. I focus on my dashboard, which gives me a summary of who has been contacted, who needs attention, and other valuable client information." She also believes communication and marketing are important. When Dawn shares valuable information, she is educating the team. They in turn can share that value with clients and prospects. All of the sales professionals' daily tasks are included in their daily plans. Everyone knows what needs to be accomplished every day.

Vision. Tony, leader and founder of a software company, talked about his critical role as a sales leader. Tony said that everyone gets complacent at one time or another. "When you are a strong leader with a positive attitude and can paint a vision for your team, you inspire people to work. I used to have new salespeople shadow the experienced people on the team, but I realized that was not the best method. People perform when they are inspired. Leaders must constantly communicate. If I don't communicate, social media and gossip will do it for me." Tony goes on to say that he lets everyone in the company know what is happening and how their part plays a big role in the success of the overall company. People feel accountable to the team. Tony continues to talk about vision and is a forward thinker. When people are educated and know what is going on, they do not question practices. Tony tells the sales professionals to never stop asking questions and listening to others' stories. Problem-solving can be visionary. Everyone can play a role in the company's future.

Tony shared a story that reflected the importance of communication and vision. He reflected on the day he knew the United States had to face an impending pandemic. He said he sat at his desk, sad. But he knew he had to fight to keep his company, employees, and his clients. He thought about Jeff Bezos talking about "going back to day one—never stop learning."

Tony said he knew that COVID-19 meant he needed to do "that old three-finger salute—control, alt, delete, and reboot." He threw away his previous thoughts about a remote workforce and called the management team together. He communicated the importance of safety and health. He planned to take care of everyone and move all of his employees to remote workplaces at home. He would make it work! After sending everyone home to safety, he communicated the new vision with so much hope and inspiration. When others see a leader who doesn't quit, it's hard for anyone to give up. He continued to paint the picture of success in a new world. And so far he is having the best year ever, with a full workforce but a very different workplace.

Motivation. Ted was the leader of a young sales team in an early stage entrepreneurial start-up. It was a niche company, and the sale was often challenging. He knew he needed to train and support his team. But it was so much more than that. One of his employees told the story of her early days with the company. She was located in a new territory, a small city outside of New York City, where Ted was based. They were hours apart, but he was always there for her. She explained that he was not checking up on her; rather, he was calling regularly to see how she was and what he could do to support her. The conversation would include the good and bad of the day, life, family, the business climate, and so much more. She explained that Ted's deep interest in everyone was a motivator. "You could see how he wanted you to be happy and succeed. At the same time, the employees were motivated to produce for themselves, their leader, and the team."

Ted said he just wanted to be there for everyone. He wanted to hear them. He wanted to keep them in the loop. He really liked his team and wanted each person to succeed. "I loved my job. And I wanted everyone else to love what they were doing," Ted mentioned twenty years later. He went on to say that he knew he had a great sales professional by their character, work ethic, and willingness to get better. These professionals saw success as the end result, and Ted felt it was his job to motivate them to get there. "I needed to hold myself accountable to being the best leader so I could watch my team succeed."

The company grew and flourished under Ted's leadership, and many years later his former employees still talk about "the boss who shaped their career."

A LOOK AT SALES IN THE POST-PANDEMIC WORLD

When written in Chinese, the word crisis is composed of two characters—one represents danger; the other represents opportunity.
—John F. Kennedy

Sales professionals have spent decades "out in the field"—building relationships, bonding, reading body language, and even entertaining. That all stopped in March of 2020. Everyone was sent home. Of course, we were hoping it would be short-lived, only a temporary break. Months later we know that many of the changes were permanent, not temporary.

So, can the sales force of today survive? Absolutely! Sales professionals are resilient. They are tough, can recover quickly, and are able to cope with change and even a crisis. But they may have to reinvent themselves to survive. We are hearing about companies that are pivoting for survival, and it appears many salespeople will need to adjust as well.

Sales professionals see opportunity. They are trained to seek opportunities. That will continue. What they will need to do is brush up on some skills, change their mindsets, and revisit their value propositions.

Let's look at what we can do to prepare to return stronger than when we left.

COMMUNICATION

Most sales professionals are good communicators. They have to use that skill. For decades, the primary communication was verbal. We talked on the phone and in person. We were warm, sometimes affectionate with handshakes and hugs and body language bonding. As time went on, we started writing more emails and even text messages. Now we will need to embrace many communication skills, including great phone skills, videoconferencing skills, and writing skills, to mention the basics. Social distancing forces a different type of bonding. It will be important to connect in other ways.

TECHNOLOGY

Although many of us have improved with respect to technology, we will now need to take another leap so we are not left behind. Many of us will be working at home (at least part of the time). That means we need to update equipment, connections, phones, databases, screens, and more. We all need to be aware of videoconferencing options and learn to sell using videoconferencing. We need to present products and services, give demos, and hold some productive conversations.

MAKE YOURSELF INTO A "BRAND"

In the next few years, at least, salespeople will not be present in offices or making regular visits. Top-of-mind awareness needs to come in other ways. It will be extremely important to have marketing support to help with visibility. It will also be important to use social media since screen time has skyrocketed in such a short span of time. It is so important to be sure that all your social media platforms are up-to-date, are accessible to searches, are professional, and make an impact. Marketing yourself as an expert, an educator, a problem solver with relevance will attract prospects. You need to offer value and solutions. You need to create opportunity. And your message must be consistent across all communication tools.

REVISIT TARGET INDUSTRIES AND TARGET MARKETS

This pandemic created new opportunities for creative business owners, and it also killed a few industries along the way. People are spending more time at home. More purchases are made online. Even our entertainment has changed. Some of the obvious industries to watch include healthcare, technology, cybersecurity, data collection, home improvements, gaming and esports. With cleanliness on the forefront, there will be a new look at clean energy, robotics, and artificial intelligence. I am sure there will be many more changes over the next several years.

EMBRACE REMOTE SELLING

Sales professionals sent home to work thought it was temporary. Many were heard saying they were going to update their database, call all of their clients, and work on their social media platforms. After a couple of weeks, it was apparent that remote selling was their only option to staying employed. Many scurried to learn videoconferencing techniques, schedule phone conferences, and write some great emails.

Now, months later, it seems that some of the workforce will be going back to their offices, but not everyone. Working remotely is here to stay. For those going back to an office, the last thing they want is an extra person from the outside. Guests, with or without masks, will not be welcomed for precautionary reasons. It is time for everyone to give the client or prospect the option of a phone or video appointment.

Great sales professionals will learn how to pivot and

adjust to remain successful. Most of them have spent many years building strong relationships within the communities and industries they serve. These people will reach out to all of their contacts and work out the best scenarios to continue to do business. The really good people will also learn how to build great online relationships using videoconferencing.

It will be very important for sales management to encourage discussions of the best sales practices, give their people the tools they need to succeed, and encourage training and self-development.

Success as a newly remote salesperson will depend on many factors. Here are a few to think about as the time to adjust is now:

- Be visible. Engage via social media, email, and text. Get involved in industry organizations and local online clubs.
- Encourage videoconferencing to keep a more "human" element. Read others' body language.
- Schedule calls and meetings. Keep a productive schedule. Set goals. Find the right routine.
- Revisit your sales process. Incorporate presentations, product visuals, and data into videoconferencing.
- Consider group webinars for better interaction between clients. Share ideas and solutions.
- Communicate. Stay on top of the process.
- Focus on results.

* * *

Changing times require changing minds.
—Unknown

The world changed drastically in a very short span of time. We were all forced to find ways to keep our businesses going while working remotely. It is amazing how people can pivot and adjust just to survive. The uncertainty we are living through adds to everyone's stress level. It will be important for sales management to support and assist. And it will be most important for sales professionals to keep up with trends, industry changes, and new technologies.

We seem to be entering a time of nationalism, "American-made," big government, and big tech. It's important to watch the trends to be a better educator and to discuss opportunities that will help clients. Sales professionals are needed to rebuild a fragile economy. They have a great opportunity to shine! Productivity, resilience, and problem-solving will be the factors that distinguish the best performers.

ACKNOWLEDGMENTS

There are so many people to thank when writing a book like this. There are the people that inspired you throughout your life—parents, mentors, past bosses, employees, and the network that supports you. I could never name all of the great people who influenced my career.

I always recommend the importance of building a strong, diverse network. I am fortunate to have two amazing clubs, the Sales Performer's Club and The Circle Leadership Group. Although I facilitate and lead these clubs, it is the members that keep me motivated to keep learning. I am so thankful to all of them for their support and excitement during this process.

My biggest thank you goes to the superstars in this book. They gave me their time and stories to make this book happen. Many of them were clients, former employees, part of my network, and just great sales professionals that I met along my journey. Not only did they share their stories, they offered sales tips and lessons that they learned "in the field." What better way to learn than to hear from these professionals directly.

Thank you to the team at Amplify Publishing, an imprint of Mascot Books, especially Nina Spahn. I was surprised and pleased that they communicated regularly with me along my journey to completion. I always knew where we were in the process and what was coming next.

One last thank you goes to my book coach, Pauline Bartel. I started this book years ago but got side tracked. Hiring a coach kept me focused and motivated. That works in sales, too!